AHA!

National Library of Canada Cataloguing in Publication Data

Parker, Barbara, 1933-
    Aha!

    ISBN 1-55212-669-2

    1. Popular culture--Psychological aspects. I. Title.
HM621.P37 2001   306'.01'9   C2001-910427-8

TRAFFORD

This book was published *on-demand* in cooperation with Trafford Publishing.
On-demand publishing is a unique process and service of making a book available for retail sale to the public taking advantage of on-demand manufacturing and Internet marketing.
On-demand publishing includes promotions, retail sales, manufacturing, order fulfilment, accounting and collecting royalties on behalf of the author.

Suite 6E, 2333 Government St., Victoria, B.C. V8T 4P4, CANADA

Phone	250-383-6864	Toll-free	1-888-232-4444 (Canada & US)
Fax	250-383-6804	E-mail	sales@trafford.com
Web site	www.trafford.com	TRAFFORD PUBLISHING IS A DIVISION OF TRAFFORD HOLDINGS LTD.	
Trafford Catalogue #01-0070		www.trafford.com/robots/01-0070.html	

10   9   8   7   6   5   4   3   2   1

AHA!

Barbara Parker

Contents

INTRODUCTION

> Know then thyself, presume not God to scan;
> The proper study of mankind is man. ...
> Sole judge of truth, in endless error hurl'd:
> The glory, jest, and riddle of the world
>
> Alexander Pope (1688 - 1744)

Modern life, for all its scientific and technological achievements, is remarkable for it being conducted largely by promptings from a hunter-gatherer brain with a little agricultural modification thrown in. We use astonishing tool-technology to stay alive longer, better, in more comfort than our neolithic forepersons. Nevertheless, as the observations and reflections collected here show, our most flourishing inventions satisfy appetites and longings which are those of the hunter-gatherer.

Although Darwin's theory of evolution had been touched upon in my high-school days, the *Beagle* and the finches got a lot more teacher-talk than did humans. That these humans need just as many generations (500+) to adapt genetically to a certain environment as do finches (500+) was definitely not on the exam. Years pass; "Genome" appears everywhere. Curious because of all the commotion surrounding this project, I sign out books from the public library whose authors theorize about who we are, what we're like, and how we got to be this way after thousands and thousands of years of evolution.

Introduction

While reading, and over time, I noticed that I said to myself (and to the cat purring on my lap[*]) "aha!" a lot. The first phase of my "aha!" moments was largely notable for the discovery that much of my behaviour did not essentially differ from that described as probable for a woman in any hunter-gatherer tribe. During the next phase I began to see myself as one speck among many specks clinging in gobs and dribbles to the surface of the globe. And soon an "aha!" escaped me because ever now and then our collective "speck" behaviour made sense where it had puzzled me before. For instance, to find a satisfying explanation for the exponentially replicating global need to own a cell-phone, all I had to do was look with my time-binoculars to a long distant past. Far, far away, our constant need to touch and to chat could be seen as behaviour perfectly adapted to conditions immemorial and pre-historic.

Putting down the binocs after having watched our evolutionary ancestors for a while, their behaviour could be observed with the naked eye—albeit concealed under all manner of high and low-tech inventions—on the street, in a mall, at a public gathering. Cars, bank machines, fast food, celebrity worship, even television were revealed as the high-tech version of some aspect of low-tech survival behaviour. AHA!'s chapters are made up of the musings over those discoveries. It is my hope that readers will, occasionally, exclaim "aha"! as well.

Before looking at some of the modern wrinkles in that ancient cloth of our make-up, one has to acknowledge that

---

[*]   see the chapter *Hair*

Introduction

modern science has discovered a thing or two about heredity. For instance, we now know that at least 500 generations have to procreate successfully (within more or less the same environment and in relative isolation) so that genetic adaptations to certain environmental conditions can take hold population-wide. That's true for no-legs fishes, six-legged fruit flies, two-legged fire-users. 500 generations means that the equivalent of "A begat B" happens approximately every 20 years in a time-span of 10,000. The new generation, the Bs, obviously again has to survive for a couple of decades to "beget" the next, the C generation. That's A begetting B, B begetting C, C begetting D, and so on, through the entire alphabet at least 21 times over! We have not even evolved sufficiently to truly get a mental handle on that long a period of time. The beginning of the Christian era, the starting date for our calendar, goes back only 100 generations.

100 generations of evolution is a spit into the winds of time. Although by our Year One settling down, tilling the soil, and domesticating animals—the beginnings of agriculture—had been "invented", food was not thought of as "daily bread" everywhere in the world. Largely, human existence was still based on gathering and hunting. Because no significant genetically encoded adaptation to changing conditions can happen in only 100 generations, our species maneuvers today in its high-tech world guided by genes still hard-wired for low-tech life in the (African) veldt. Whatever fed body and soul then is what exerts a powerful appeal today. Our inclinations and responses are the same still. Although clothed in the fused double-layer of "modernity & progress",

Introduction

the neurology underneath is that of the pre-agricultural tribe person.

That same primitive in me hollered "aha!" when I discovered that the predispositions of my fellow primitives turned out to be the bedrock upon which so many of the wildly successful, the global marketplace conquering consumer items are built. The success of television, 24/7 weather channels, big box stores, three-tenor-concerts, the mouse-click is thriving proof of needs splendidly satisfied today but evolved for conditions long past. We're coded still as standard issue of our ancestors who—and that's important—only are our ancestors because their wiring stood the test: the successful survival of their DNA.

Evolution is not only a very long but also an incredibly slow process. For hundreds of thousands of years our evolutionary ancestors picked up sticks and stones and used them as tools. Eventually humans thought a few steps ahead to the task to be done, picked a specific stone, modified it so it could be used, for instance, to scrape an animal skin free of the meat. By not just letting the meat rot off it, they made more efficient use of the hide. That's primitive technology, but it's technology. Technology is our forte. However, even if tech change takes a few hundreds years to percolate through populations, we only *adapt* (by means of an evolving but not necessarily enduring culture) to what we invent; we do not *evolve* genetically alongside the invention.

Whether inventing a stone-axe or finessing the cell-phone, humans have a propensity to make things that bring

Introduction

gratifying results immediately. We have a hard time giving thought to the long-term consequences our use of those brainchildren might have because until less than 100 years ago we didn't live long enough to have to suffer possible consequences. An average life span to age 35 for thousands of years does not teach a lesson to the cutter of the first two dozen—and not re-seeded—trees of a seemingly never-ending forest. The kind of myopia bemoaned today regarding matters environmental has not had time enough, or conditions sufficiently favourable, to evolve out of us. Short life-spans over eons have not let us evolve into far-sighted, instinctive planners who would factor in, let's say, the next five generations.

It used to be that every technological change was slow in coming, and another would not appear until way beyond a single human life-span. One of those first homo sapiens sapiens made life more pleasant by deliberately choosing material that could be given an "eye" through which a filament could be threaded. That first sewing needle dates to approximately 22,000 years ago. A needle-wielder then would have had to stick around for another 12,000 years to enjoy the benefits that came with deliberately warping and woofing animal hair to weave into a piece of cloth.

In the chapters that follow, our shortsightedness will be taken for granted and not lamented. AHA! describes what is; it does not opine as to what "ought" to be. It is a collection of amazed glimpses at our ingenuity in creating the most intriguing tool-toys while conforming to some prehistoric survival behaviour. Although stand-alone chapters, they lead

Introduction

toward an inescapable conclusion: over the last 35,000 years or so we have not evolved significantly from the person who lived in the midst of a tribe in the veldt or the cave. We do use our astonishing brain capacity, however, to invent and use technology to live like our pre-historic foreparents but with almost magically greater ease and comfort. In short, we blithely stride ahead while still dragging our Cro-Magnon umbilical cord behind us.

The Packrat

> A bird in the hand is worth two
> in the bush.
>
> Ancient Proverb

Long before we were a twinkle in evolution's eye, those
precursors whose genetic imprint we share—fish-reptile-
bird-mammal—instinctively stuffed themselves when good
luck or skill presented them with more than they needed to
still the hunger of the moment. Most animals hide, bury,
store food against a rainy day. Most animals eat all they
possibly can during times of plenty, store fat on their bodies,
and live off this provision during lean times. The human
animal grabs what it can while it can, employing its fearfully
well developed cerebral cortex. We can't alter this coding
for hoarding even though environment and circumstance are
no longer those of the days without shopping channels. And
so it is that we pounce with joyful abandon upon the
abundance of the marketplace. We get our high from
acquisition, and contentment from our collections. As a
hoarder, the human leaves the packrat and the squirrel in the
dust.

We're wired to react to the slightest suspicion that rough
times might lurk just around the corner! For the very best of
reasons, our built-in alarm system catapults us into action at
the merest hint of deprivation. That reason lies in our
evolutionary past. Being prepared for bad times served us
well from the time humans budded as another branch on the
bush of species. But another instinct, the one to wield tools

and to invent, has led to a fantastical ornamentation of that most basic impulse to want to possess more than two sticks to rub together. To want the better mousetrap—and to procure three to be on the safe side—is an impulse satisfied by our remarkable ingenuity. Our consumer culture flowers so abundantly because that ingenuity dove-tails with the hoarding instinct from long before the dawn of man.

These habits from a deep-time past propel us to be content only when we possess a stash of stuff. Free of the fear that the life-sustaining herd of reindeer might move elsewhere, proud of our ability to think rationally, blessed with a shopping emporium always within driving distance, we nevertheless cannot shake the thinking of our far off ancestors. The impulse to hoard, originally adaptive behaviour which, over time, became genetically encoded, has not had time to wither away. The store(house) down the street has been with us for no more than 150 years, a mere six generations. That's not enough time gone by to know as a bedrock certainty that there is some place, somewhere, within driving distance, open 24/7, where one can exchange money for food.

The prudent hoarder, who did better at having her/his DNA survive than the unprovisioned human, is plentifully represented in populations everywhere. In the appliance-rich countries, for instance, one finds that a certain ice-cave allure attaches to the freezer. Into its pit one crams chicken @ 23cents/lb for which one expended $10 in time, gas and car depreciation. Freezer packages are either not labeled or labels have come off or they're illegible or they read "May

The Packrat

12" (no year). The bottom layer has not been seen in 5 years!

"This will come in handy one day" coding seems to be the darling imprint of DNA! This is one of those fine abstract statements which we recognize as having considerable footing in reality. To get away from the abstraction, to really get a handle on what we are prone to do, have done, do still, see being done, laugh at, shake our heads over, recognize in ourselves, a few very concrete illustrations are in order.

For instance, the prudent person's hoarder mechanism clicks into gear when guessing at some value at some time for the still intact rubber glove for the left hand. Throw it out? Naaa! Might come in handy! Put it in this (stuffed) drawer. Prudent hoarder vaguely recalls that about three other left-hand rubber gloves live in some drawer(s) or other. Well, all this stuff will get organized one day!

Prudent hoarder person tends to live in a place where the car is parked on the street because the garage is full of stuff. The stuff in the garage is actually the overflow from the stuff in the basement. The stuff in the basement accumulated because space had to be freed up from cupboards that spilled their contents upon opening and drawers that could no longer be closed. The overflow from cupboards and drawers was first, unsuccessfully, stored in the spare room or in "organizers" under the beds, or in boxes ... supposedly temporary measures all.

The Packrat

Take note: The next section is only for those readers who feel superior to the Prudent Person Hoarder and believe themselves immune to the entreaties of the squirrel in us.

That brilliant bit of stash-coding for survival lies completely outside our rational control. Here then, because two concrete examples are worth eleven abstractions (the manipulation of abstractions not yet being our strong point), more glimpses on what we folks collect:

- ∽ rolled-up as well as loose bits of various kinds of string mixed in with small paper bags intermingled with fridge magnets, a broken hook, paper clips, 2 washed but frayed dish-rags, plastic cutlery odds & sods, elastics (some snapped), 21 coupons (all expired), a bottle of dried-up plant fertilizer ... in a kitchen drawer
- ∽ recipe books, recipe clippings, copied recipes, recipe hand-outs, recipes on the back of tin labels, recipes from the back of cereal boxes ... two life-times' worth of cooking a different dish every single day!
- ∽ 146 bits and pieces of such Mr. Fix-It stuff as various lengths of 2 x 4s and 1 x 2s, plywood, lath, molding, doweling, particle board, laminated leavings from installing the kitchen counter, 3 cedar shingles, odd pieces of wall-paneling, 1 fence post, 9 "found" odd lengths and widths of shelving ... along two walls in the basement
- ∽ the handy person's collection of plumbing remnants: washers, slip nuts, pipe tape, an assortment of old ball cocks, a generous helping of valves, tubing, lengths of

pipe, a hank of oakum and, just in case, an arsenal of *used* trap bends … in a semi-collapsed cardboard box

↬ dull pencils and dried-out ballpoint pens, drinking straws, 2 wooden skewers, paper clips, swizzle sticks from spirited evenings out ... in several broken handled mugs

↬ empty & washed plastic ice-cream, margarine, yogurt, bleach, honey, bottled water, deli, fridge/freezer containers … a truly awesome collection

↬ t-shirts, sweat-shirts, polo-shirts, casual shirts, under shirts, dress shirts, ultralite polyprop shirts, blazer shirts, heavy-duty checkered work shirts, tank tops ... in various colours, styles, sizes, fabrics (most of them unfashionable as well as too small for our ripened body!)

↬ the flotsam of our existence in any shape, colour, size: vases, cutlery, bubble-wrap, stuffed animals, 3 shelves of recorded music tapes, soap remnants, dolls, cushions, souvenirs, bowls, artificial flowers, paraphernalia hung on walls, print between covers and loose on diverse surfaces, knickknacks, live plants, dead plants, pretty bowls, used plastic bags, half-full bottles of shampoo, toys for the dog, toys for the baby, 8 partially recorded video tapes without labels, 11 bottles of once-used nail polish, many lipsticks from fashions past, gap-toothed combs, 2 lamps that don't work, that second-hand golf set

↬ a couple of receptacles full of keys? Really! A heap of keys constitutes the most enigmatic treasure of our packratism. The hoarder-owner, in 99.99% of all dwellings with items that are lockable, is unable to remember which key fits which lock. Whether the keys are in a dish, in a box, labeled (hardly ever), labeled (seldom decipherable), cropping up hither and or thither, needing bringing together or not, they endure beyond house moves, door replacements, changes of locks, a succession of cars, a succession of mates, a succession of bicycle anti-theft devices, replaced or lost luggage, the sale of the antique wind-up clock.

The almost absent-minded (not to call it *irrational*) putting aside of the odds and sods of daily life which may save a trip to the store or prevent flooding of the bathroom floor is a template in the human brain which generates many off-spring. One child of this predisposition to stashing has segued nicely from the uncharted ebb and flow of life within the home world into the supposedly rational and flow-charted business world.

Even in these surroundings —ever so far removed from the African veldt where it all began —the impulse to protect against the seven lean years is given rein with enthusiasm. Every memo, every letter, every directive, every report gets photocopied x times, attached to a circulation slip with tick-off boxes, and sent on its way. Some of the tick-persons photocopy "it" again, to be sent on yet another circuit. That same chunk of information is on someone's hard drive, maybe on a floppy, in an IN or OUT basket, somewhere in a "to be-filed" heap. One fears the day on which this very bit of information would come in handy to nourish a room full of fact-starved colleagues.

The Packrat

Anyone who has worked, however briefly, in a large office has observed residual packrat habits in and around the toilers' lair. One can never have enough of the ubiquitous paper clip; it serves as the ultimate security blanket. Top desk drawers are one quarter full of spent as well as new writing implements. In that same desk can be found stacks of message pads, some from before voice mail; veritable nests of miscellaneously sized rubber bands; a box of crackers well past the best-before date; socks, kleenex, 3 combs, emery boards, tea bags, various brands of pain killers; one fresh eraser and two hardened and black with age, bottles with dried-out correction fluid; the odd bright ribbon from an office present ... and many more items of a nature best kept quiet about.

Our coding from long ago is equally observable in the boardroom where the entire hunter-gatherer behaviour unfolds before our eyes. In today's corporate world the object is not the woolly mammoth, but the whole enterprise. In merger mania times predominantly male heads of companies follow a combination of ancient codes: searching out, hunting down, stunning, then killing the prey, partaking of the fresh liver or heart, schlepping the carcass to the home cave, stripping it down, eating some, hoarding lots. Deep satisfaction, however fleeting, results in beholding a big, beautiful pile of meat and bones, a merger-pile of previous and present kills.[*]

---

[*] Let the annals of the 20th century hunt give pride of place to T. Boone Pickens, someone who lived up to his name as chaser & acquisitor in the 1970s.

The Packrat

From the exalted enlarging of the pile which, after all, does contain "real" estate and commodities, to the mandated collection of data in vast banks of information, the notion is never far off that "it" may be, will be, needed one day. The information age has not brought with it one iota of change in hoarding behaviour. The idea of "having", that is "possessing", information black on white, or squirreled away electronically, has brought with it a curious correlative. The act of having and storing information somehow confers importance, veracity, worth because we reassure ourselves that should the need arise, it's there to be understood, known, internalized, made use of, profited by. Having is all: seldom is the eager "may I have this to make a copy for myself?" followed by a sit-down meal of reading and digesting!

The reality is that simply "having" the piece of information or knowing where it is stored is of as little use as is one of those stashed-away household items. When we need the thingamabob, we can't find it; we go out instead and buy a new one. When the call goes out for specific information, seldom is it remembered *what* was filed *when* or *where*. Nor has that organizer's dream, the multi giga-byte hard drive, changed our antediluvian packrat functions. Everyone with a computer recognizes these treasures: folders with a couple of files in them; files strewn all over the Windows Explorer; files, their names forgotten, can't be found with the "Find" command; wads of e-mails, sent and received and deleted, compacted already 4 x; seven game demos = boooooooring but not deleted. This precious hoard—for gosh's sake—got copied onto the zip drive or burnt into a CD while doing a system's back-up.

The Packrat

The elite of the packrats is the hobby collector. The focused, often high-minded, in any event earnest collector spends time and/or money on a broadly or narrowly defined assortment of anything that can be collected, categorized, indexed, and displayed: books, cars, comics, Barbie dolls, out-dated TV sets, belt buckles, matchbooks, paintings, guns, candlesticks, works of art, Hummel figurines, crystal, anything homely, anything glittery, anything ephemeral, anything eternal = any "thing".

In a category all by itself is the collector of zeros. He/she tends to be admired, envied, emulated most. They amass, bit by bit, whatever represents the great abstraction, that which is nothing unless their tribe has assigned value to it, that which is considered currency. Whether colourful pebbles, pieces of gold, sea shells, paper, or computer entries, no matter what we ingenious monkeys decide on, we collect a *representation* of value. Fairy tales, myths, theatre pieces deal with misers who forget why it is that they save and thereby forget to live life. Who knows not a person who "collects" money without really being able to say what the money will be useful for? Ironically, what is being collected is, literally, the next ZERO. And it doesn't matter whether that zero is added on to a 1, a 10, or a 100000; the thrill is the same.

Hoarding, much like having sex, is an activity that preserves the individual and the species. Like having sex, hoarding is intensely pleasurable while indulging, and it leaves the same glow of satisfaction. For a brief moment, one feels at peace with oneself and the world. Sexual images sell goods because mating and providing for survival are bedrock, that is, mother-board wiring. The appeal to these basic urges and their gratification—preferably immediate—has been kicked into high gear by modern technology. Our instinct to hoard pretty well anything and everything has made the triumph of the consumer society inevitable.

Laying by a stash of dried fish for the winter has morphed into the sheer accumulation of "stuff" all year round. The stuff is not long-lived. Not only is most of what we buy obsolete before a twentieth of a lifetime has passed, but more and more of the acquisitions vanish almost the hour they are bought. Brand K is history; long live brand Q! Been there; done that; got the T-shirt! Watched five videos over the weekend ... awesome! Fourth set of cooking pots at age 39.

> ⇒ **consume**, v.
> 1. to destroy or expend by use; use up
> 2. to eat or drink up; devour
> 3. to spend wastefully

Third set of golf-clubs though game has yet to improve. Let's go for a drive, to a factory outlet for designer clothes. A third cordless phone. 11 CDs on special for $29.99. New mugs, watering can, 7-in-1 screwdriver, 2 action figures, handycam, curling iron. Have a garage sale. Return to Start.

However, Start and Finish are no longer separated by a straight line. Instead both points lie on a circle and are hard to pin-point. We consume the natural resources of our environment to keep the consumer society going which, in turn, keeps an enormous population employed which, in turn, goes on consuming so it can be employed so it can survive.

The Packrat

This hamster on his wheel exertion is an unintended consequence of how our minds evolved. Our minds evolved to deal with a world and living conditions utterly unlike those prevailing today. Our minds are still functioning in that mode because

1. not enough time with its requisite number of generations has passed to let behaviour evolve to fit the world created by our inventions;

2. we can and do change our environment to fit our behaviour which precludes the environment forcing the change upon us.

Gobbling and hoarding being in our genes, a branch of consumerism, marketing, works best when it can tweak that packrat grid in our cerebral cortex. Marketers <u>do</u> lie awake at night, thinking up ways to get us to trade our money against a doodad. And we respond. As it happens, all modern merchandising clicks into our wiring in some form or another. We consumers, by our enthusiastic response, feed with coin and keep alive the Sale, the Supermarket, the Mall, and the Big Box Store. What follows shows how we fit those inventions and how those inventions fit us.

The **SALE** —
Advertised as lasting only from Tuesday to Monday, it combines the notion of a bargain with the terrorizing thought that one might lose out by

- not being there before the goods have disappeared
- not being able to hoard during the times of plenty, that is Tuesday to Monday

- not being there to get something more easily, that is, more cheaply.

This in turn leads to households harbouring five boxes of laundry detergent; 96 rolls of toilet paper; a 20-can box of pea soup but a brand that nobody likes; 3 family packs (10 each & taking up too much space in the fridge freezer) of chicken drumsticks for which a tolerable recipe cannot be found; 2 blouses (too small) that were the price of one; a set of saw-blades @ 65% off but, as it turns out, the wrong gauge for the saw one owns; great runners for half price but one size too large and which no amount of socks will make serviceable.

The **Super Market** —

As the name implies this market, above and beyond, *super*ior to all markets, appeals to our most basic instincts for survival because there's

- food in abundance (hoard, hoard; privation lurks!)
- food displayed to catch the eye (grab, grab; we respond to bright colours!)
- food made easy to gather (the basket is on wheels!)
- food bundled for us to take to our dwelling (stash, stash; feel rich!)

The **Mall** —

The naming of this roof-covered assemblage of shopping opportunities was a brilliant stroke of putting an old-tech meaning to a new-tech concept. The feel-good aspect of the word nicely camouflaged the changed nature of our outings. Not that long ago the word "mall" referred to "a large area, usually lined with shade trees and shrubbery, used as public

The Packrat

walkway or promenade". Today's mall, lined with stores, artificially lit, decorated with counterfeit or extremely hardy greenery, is the morphed tundra and glade, woodland and the river bank. Here the gatherer in us roams, filling (plastic) containers with "unearthed" bargains. As in those ancient times, the female of the species likes to do her gathering in groups, at the very least in twosomes. Matrons shop with a friend; ♀ teenagers roam in small cliques; mothers teach their daughters about good value; adult daughters treat their aged mother to an outing. Males, as they were in pre-historic times, are seen here only with women at the stage of boyhood or in their second infancy. Thus ♂ teenagers come to malls to hang out and only very incidentally to shop; adult males are seen very rarely and if, they do a kind of "hang-back" walk; and geezer males drift from bench to bench in search of someone to tell tall tales to.

The **Big Box Store** —
This is the packrats' paradise. However, unlike the paradisiacal environment known from the great myth, this one is found in overwhelming cement cubes. The very shape suggests a container full of goodies in which one is allowed to rummage at will. Nevertheless, the territory for the intended activity is of proportions suitable for provisioning entire tribes of yore.

The big box store presents our nervous system with the most bang for our buck. A shopping expedition to the outskirts of town lets us combine infatuation with the car and passion for possessions. Once we get there, the age-old hunting & gathering instincts take over. The hunter in all of us goes for the biggest animal (it offers, after all, the largest meat supply), while the gatherer collects as many edibles as can be found in one outing (to eat some and to store what's left). Guaranteed ample parking welcomes the provider for home and hearth. The sustaining territory inside the box is a vast field with row upon row of shelves packed with pickings. Bin upon bin filled with stuff dot this landscape like big, ripe, seed-spilling fruit. An emotional high comes with the absolute certainty that one is saving gobs and gobs of money. Deep satisfaction warms one's heart while in the midst of this throng of like-minded practitioners. The sensation of being part of some larger purpose is deeply satisfying. Finally, the ease of wheeling the pickings to the car is nicely enhanced by a feeling of virtuousness. One has acted smartly to stave off hunger and want. This calls for a reward! Make the foray a total experience and grab some fast food on the way home.

Destination shopping is much like destination worshipping. The tithing has been replaced by the yearly membership fee. This membership immediately sets the member apart from the non-member, creating that nice warm feeling of belonging to an exclusive group, partaking of an activity for the person of good judgment. Although organized religion with its ritualized services—which makes the believer get up, dress for public view, reach the destination church, engage in a satisfying common enterprise, feel a member of a community, mingle socially—has fallen on hard times, it is not the activity that has lost its attraction, it is the venue which has lost its drawing power. In times of material

The Packrat

plenty, the hoarding of things for the body has replaced the hoarding of merits for the soul.

Our culture may change, the packrat in us does not.

THE GENETIC FLUKE

> Then one day a prince was
> traveling through the land.

Not that the environment doesn't matter! But for fame and
riches it's essential that somewhere along the double helix
there be something special, something that gives the carrier
what we call a "talent" or "gift".   And so it is a gift!
Unearned, unsought, cannot be bought.   This fluke in the
genetic assembly line can make for a body extraordinarily
quick of eye, fleet of foot, strong of arm, golden-voiced,
nimble-fingered. Not in mythical times nor today does such
a person have to fret about status, acolytes, or vittles. The
rest of us folk admire and love and reward the flukes with
high status because something in us feels good about that
special gene in our pool.

Our ancestors already showered with high esteem and with
whatever acceptable currency that out-of-the-ordinary gene
configuration, be it the peerless hunter or gatherer, the knight
who could swing the meanest sword, or the spinster[*] whose
thread was the finest, most even, and seldom broke. Today's
warrior in the sports arena, the conquering CEO, the virtuoso
of the domestic arts is the one who is treated handsomely by
us, the humans surrounding the genius. Those who stand out
from the masses in today's field of action—be that
entertainment, dot-commery, the stock market, sports, the

---

[*]   "spinster" is here used in its original sense of "a woman whose
occupation is spinning"

media—are offered multi-million dollar contracts, stock-options, bonuses, golden-parachutes, and/or their own TV show with the product tie-in not far behind. All are granted celebrity status. High-tech has enormously embellished the reward structure for the high-achiever.

If not fame or fortune, at the very least a comfortable living is assured any child born with physical or mental gifts. These off-spring shine where others bumble or are merely adequate. The metaphorical dragon slayer getting the metaphorical hand of the princess and living in splendour ever after—while the crowds shout the equivalent of "way to go"—is alive and doing better than ever. While the fastest running and most unerringly spear-throwing hunter was immortalized in tribal tales or in paintings on a cave wall, we have ratcheted up adulation of the genetically privileged quite a few notches. We reward the genetic fluke if he or she exhibits specific qualities deemed desirable because they fit into our environment, that of the 3rd millennium.

So it is that we common folk admire the personages for what's been handed them by the gods. They are known, like brand merchandise, for what they do so exceedingly well. We pay the price asked for the consumption of their "product", a "product" that cannot be manufactured on the assembly line. Some of these known and loved assets (in every way) to the gene pool are: The Three Tenors, The Face the Camera Loves, The Bosom, The World-Class Athlete, The Entrepreneurial Mind-Grid, The Story Spinner, The Domestic Paragon, The One Conversant With Computers.

The Genetic Fluke

In a manner of speaking, everyone of us is a genetic fluke. Everyone—unless an identical twin—has some tiny bit of DNA- coding no one else has. If this weren't so, DNA testing would not be the unique identifier it is. If this weren't so, evolution would not be the proposition that it is. Evolution depends on heritable advantages—which one organism has and another in the same environment does not—being selected precisely because they are useful, that is, they are not selected at random. Without diversity evolution cannot produce better adapted organisms. Every now and then something really quite different has to be thrown up, something that is, by an accidental stroke of gene formation, coded to perform faster, higher, wider, in a more complex way within—again—the environment it finds itself.

We call the accidentally advantaged ones "stars". That says a lot about how we view those whose physical prowess, artistic talent, business acumen, external beauty illuminates an otherwise common experience. Billions of night sky stars provide the vast back-drop for the trajectory of a few brilliant editions. The top illuminators look beautiful and intrigue us. Without them the sky would not look half as handsome. The star-sky analogy holds also in that some stars appear briefly, flicker brightly, then flame out. The genetic fluke we look up to, celebrate, whose every move we're interested in is the one who embodies in a greatly enhanced mode an otherwise common characteristic or competence in us, the lesser lights.

Consider singing. All of us can sing. But it is the fluke whose voice box is shaped by that extra bit of special coding

The Genetic Fluke

that makes for musicality outside the norm. When we hear that voice, the way it carries, soars, caresses, plays with a melody, is perfectly pitched, we get goosebumps. Tears threaten to well in our eyes when we hear that effortless high C, that tight-rope display of something we cannot do even if we dedicated our life to the pursuit. We show our admiration with lots of physical movement—a sure sign that we have to work off arousal in the brain/soul. Even in so august a setting as an opera house and attired in finery, we jump from our seats, stomp, yell "bravo, bravo" or emit other loud noises, and beat our hands together to make yet more noise. It has been known to happen that audiences get carried away in their enthusiasm and indulge their frenzy for longer than it took to sing the aria in the first place.

Opera is as good a field as any to illustrate a verity: even among the flukes shine hyper-flukes. Among the three tenors we focus on Pavarotti. Luciano seems to have something which his two buddies lack. Despite his corpulence in an age that's fixated on being in (thin) shape, the "Pav" has become a household word. Pavarotti's appeal is not something he somehow "deserved" more than the other tenors of his generation. Domingo and Carreras look fitter, for one thing. But there's something irresistible about Pavarotti's physicality: the face that exudes ruddy health, the thousand watt smile, the teddy-bear eyes, that non-threatening vitality. Not a single trait among them that he laboured to acquire.

The "Pav" would have been revered and, consequently, been well off during cave or village times. Today though, the village is global and our technology can boost his recognition factor and income to stratospheric heights. But how we react today is not different from how small populations regarded those whose labours produced more useful or more beautiful results. Those who excelled beyond what mere practice and determination can accomplish, whether hunters, gatherers, fighters, tool makers, story tellers, cloth felters, needle wielders, shamans, or artists, would have been favoured by the collective. The high esteem in which the maker of the best mousetrap was held tended to throw its sheen on other endeavours he undertook (in most arenas of life it was a "he"). If a person is good at something in one area, we tend to think that they must be just as "smart" in another. Tribes elect their best hunter as their leader. Yet nowhere is it written that such a person is also wise in the ways of governance. Nothing much has changed. As technology makes it easy to live once more the tribal life[*], our electing of authority figures and leaders favours those whose genetic composition made them successful elsewhere. To have been a star in movies, in the wrestling ring, or in the space program seems to us proof enough that we can trust this person to do the right thing for the public good.

Before public health measures were instituted and the resulting low infant mortality became a reality, the chance for survival of the genetically favoured's progeny was higher than for the children born to the lowly clan member. When grown, the offspring often inherited the power-mantle because—even without the benefit of the systematic study of

---

[*] see "Print is Toast", the last chapter

The Genetic Fluke

genetics—greatness was thought to beget greatness or, at the very least, some talent would rub off. Here we are in the 21st century and our minds, still running in the tribal mode, are comfortable with the idea that dad/mom talent begets daughter/son talent. The number of children of successful politicians, movie stars, business conglomerate owners emerging as "natural" successors and being elected, adulated, rewarded by the rest of us is astonishing. Even relatives of the gifted ones get to bask in reflected glory. We cannot, in good conscience, say that we treat the occurrence of the fluke rationally. To those at the other end of the genetic lottery, the losers, we barely grant charity. Local or global village, nothing's changed because we've not changed.

Our undying admiration for those who do things we can do, only ever so much better, is laid at the feet of another fluke in our time, the undisputed doyenne of domesticity, Martha Stewart. Her books are huge bestsellers, her magazine boasts excellent circulation figures, her television program never lacks for sponsors or viewers. Recently she incorporated herself and after the IPO figures were in, lo! Martha was a billionairess. The law of identification, as it is with singing, is here at work as well. We all know, sort of, how to decorate a table! Yeah, but we just wouldn't think up a table centre-piece crafted of carrot greens with animal shapes carved from beet root cavorting beneath the fronds. We love and imitate and pay for Martha's fluke-ish ability to accessorize, organize, glamorize. She hits the impossibly high notes on the scale of domesticity.

The Genetic Fluke

It is, however, in that still largely male domain, the sports arena, where more rapidly firing synapses or genetically favoured muscle arrangements set off wild shouts of joy and/or undomesticated behaviour. Long before super athletes could be seen on television, in the dark ages, audiences watched "stars" half in fascination, half in awe as they produced those thrills that cause heart palpitations, occasionally even fainting spells. One can guess at the excitement produced during the great jousting tournaments of the 12th century. They were so popular that successive popes forbade them but to no avail. The knight who could lance an opponent off his horse while in full gallop and perform this feat over and over was, no doubt, a star in every sense of our use of the word. His reflexes, coupled to general prowess, were every bit as unusual as Wayne Gretzky's "210° field of vision" or "the magic" of Johnson is today. Because of his wizardly scoring powers, Earvin got re-christened "Magic". His genetic fluke-ness shows in that he's graceful, superbly coordinated and, at 6'9", the tallest guard in league history. Neither Gretzky nor Johnson can be emulated by merely practicing around the clock or getting the right kinds of vitamins while in nursery school.

If greatness in sports could be attained for expending effort and partaking of micro-nutrients, the allure of the sports star and the resulting adrenaline rush in the audience would be no more. Equally gone would be the social mobility which attends the settling out of the genetic fluke. In the Middle Ages, for instance, the repeatedly victorious knight was rewarded with a noble's daughter's hand, a rich purse, and chunks of land. Today the fluke-ish sports hero is rewarded

The Genetic Fluke

with a multi-million dollar contract, another bunch of millions through endorsements, thereby guaranteeing that he can buy pretty well whatever the knight was handed and attract today's princess, the celeb screen-star or run-way model. Knight-time, because it favoured a superb rider, a strong swinging arm, excellent hand-eye coordination, brought to the fore boys even if they came from indentured stock. Once spotted as promising material, they were put in training under the lord's protection and thereby on their way up the social ladder. They became landed gentry. In our time "gifted" kids in the ghettos are spotted, then sponsored, then rewarded because what they were born with happens to let them slam-dunk what we—King Public—value inordinately.

Whether in our cave past, during the days of knightly combat, or in the electronic universe, one pre-condition prevails before we grant elevation and adulation to those few among us. Then as now we have to be able to identify with the fluke's gift. In fact, the easier the identification, the higher the reward. We can all sing, so singers of all kinds are high on the scale of glorification. We can all run and throw a ball. We all look in the mirror and make faces; we all have best and worst body features. So, naturally, we admire to the point of awe those who can sing, run, throw, act, be beautiful so exhilaratingly better than we can. Michael Jackson is mega-rich because he combines singing and dancing. Then there's Michael Flatley! No other pop dancer has recently garnered the kind of success and sincerest form of flattery, imitation, than this fluke combo of lightning fast feet[*], fevered choreographic inspiration, and impresario-smarts. We bestow success because—evidence to the contrary—we cannot but help harbour the sneaking suspicion that, given determination, practice, support, we too could dance almost like that.

In contrast, we do not reward in the same way those whose giftedness we cannot readily identify with. These winners sparkle against a different firmament. Although occasionally one of these shining lights gets to go super nova, by and large the physicist, mathematician, geographer, philosopher, architect, engineer, composer, painter, choreographer has a harder time to conclude million-dollar contracts than the dude in the arena or in show business. As well, our collective favours and bestows the richest rewards upon the male fluke because we're still running with a very old operating system.

That OS under-pinning our behaviour can run some entertaining but also instructive programs. The tale of the sleeping beauty who is awaked by a prince from far away is such a program. In electronic terms it means that the old code gets sort of freshened up and that something new may even be generated. With us 21st century humans the program tells us not only to tolerate culturally and visibly different persons but also to mate with them. This is nothing new and we've been prepared to set aside our distrust of the stranger—albeit a special stranger—for a long, long time.

---

[*] Evidently his feet can "produce" 28 clicks per second!

The Genetic Fluke

A band or tribe, hunting and gathering more than a five days' journey away from others of its kind, lives an isolated existence. It will need new blood every few generations. So it is that fairytales and myths galore follow the pattern in which an enervated, static, or endangered realm is invigorated or saved by a male outsider, invariably handsome of mien, noble of character, and talented in wielding weapons. Observe that the snatching of neighbouring females, though evidently common in real life, does not dot the myth-scape. Rather, the infusion of new DNA into a population via the heroic, the handsome, the one that "makes the difference" seems to have taken hold. Myths and fairytales **are** instructive. Which is why *Sleeping Beauty* bears looking at in the light of what we know about DNA, the need for diversity, and genetic flukes.

SLEEPING BEAUTY

A king and queen had no children, although they wanted one very much.
After about 150 generations (3,000 years) of in-breeding, the top couple have a hard time reproducing.
Then one day a daughter was born. The king was so happy about the birth of the princess that he held a great celebration.
Celebrating is justified. Half a DNA loaf is better than no loaf at all.
He invited the fairies who lived in his kingdom, but because he had only twelve golden plates, one fairy had to be left out, for there were thirteen of them.

The Genetic Fluke

Good example of administrative rules sapping the strength of common sense! So what #13 has to eat off pewter? (Another indication that the sweeping of a new broom would do some good!)

The fairies ... presented the child with virtue, beauty, and so on, each one offering something desirable and magnificent.

We get to know that the child's DNA is not to be sneezed at.

The thirteenth fairy walked in, very angry, and cried out, "Because you did not invite me, I tell you that in her fifteenth year, your daughter will prick herself with a spindle and fall over dead."

Bang on puberty, this young woman will hurt herself on a distaff implement and die. That'll be really the end of this particular strain of DNA.

The twelfth fairy, who had not yet offered her wish, said, "It shall not be her death. She will only fall into a hundred-year sleep."

Commutation to 100 years of "not having a life" (which is mod speak for "not having any dates or not being in a relationship", therefore not doing that which reproduces ...)

The king ... had all spindles in the entire kingdom destroyed.

Nice shot at modifying the environment!

The princess grew and became a miracle of beauty.

Good! Perfect phenotype.

One day, in her fifteenth year, the king and queen being away, the princess investigated the entire castle. ... She came upon an old woman spinning flax. Trying her hand at spinning, the princess pricked herself with the spindle and then fell down into a deep sleep.

Not even the study of the domestic arts is sufficient to keep this enervated royal issue "alive".

At that same moment the king and his attendants returned, and everyone began to fall asleep: the horses in the stalls, the pigeons on the roof, the dogs in the courtyard, the flies on the walls. Even the fire on the hearth flickered, stopped moving, and fell asleep. The roast stopped sizzling. The cook let go of the kitchen boy, whose hair he was about to pull. The maid dropped the chicken that she was plucking. They all slept. And a thorn hedge grew up around the entire castle, growing higher and higher, until nothing at all could be seen of it.

A weakened bloodline leads to somnambulant behaviour which leads to the eventual invisibility of the entire ruling house.

Princes, who had heard about the beautiful Briar-Rose, came and tried to free her, but they could not penetrate the hedge. The princes became stuck in them, and they died miserably. And thus it continued for many long years.

What's required here is one of the species but with a slight gene mutation which confers thorn-bush-fighting-and-conquering capabilities.

Then one day a prince was traveling through the land. An old man told him about the belief that there was a castle behind the thorn hedge, with a wonderfully beautiful princess asleep inside with all of her attendants. His grandfather had told him that many princes had tried to penetrate the hedge, but that they had gotten stuck in the thorns and had been pricked to death.

Generations pass. The kingdom lies inactive. Consultants from elsewhere are rendered impotent.

"I'm not afraid of that," said the prince. "I shall penetrate the hedge and free the beautiful Briar-Rose."

Atta boy! Heroic genotype. Knows no fear and trusts himself to go where no man has gone before.

He went forth, but when he came to the thorn hedge, it turned into flowers.

Genetic fluke: what others perceive as thorns, the prince sees as flowers. Leaps tall buildings in a single bound, etc.

...

He walked through ... and finally came to the old tower where Briar-Rose was lying asleep. The prince was so amazed at her beauty that he bent over and kissed her.

A condensed and restrained way of conveying what really happened.

At that moment the princess awoke, and with her the king and the queen, and all the attendants, and the horses and the dogs, and the pigeons on the roof, and the flies on the walls. The fire stood up and flickered, and then finished cooking the food. The roast sizzled away. The cook boxed the kitchen boy's ears. And the maid finished plucking the chicken.

In-migration and inter-marriage restore vigour to a debilitated strain of DNA.

The Genetic Fluke

Then the prince and Briar-Rose got married, and they lived long and happily until they died.
The alpha male has come from afar, succeeded where others failed, and secured the highest prize. New DNA emerges while preserving that which characterizes the tribe/realm.

The global village does what a village has always done: although generally suspicious and resentful of outsiders, it will jubilate and celebrate and take to its collective heart the one that is, or seems, outstandingly different from the locals. This is the first step to letting new blood into the tribe. In our tech-besotted world our entertainment choices easily snap into one or more of our ancient notches. Shows displaying the fluke-ishly endowed Pamela Anderson succeed wildly and widely. Banknotes flutter to her and to those who market her. *Baywatch* is seen in 110+ countries around the globe every day. And not a single viewer has been reported as having had to be hand-cuffed to the TV set!

Martha Stewart's territory management, Michael Jackson's double-jointed dancing, Bill Gates' marketing genius, Stephen Hawkins' brain emanations, Michael Jordan's exploits in the ball court fit nicely into our synaptic circuit spot where we long to be more than we are. The paleolithic tribal instinct to set apart and ensure that the best hunter, the best tool-maker, the best food preserver be singled out and rewarded to ensure a whole bunch of offspring—among whom at least a couple of reasonably accurate copies might emerge—is still firmly in us. It's in our bones that we pay homage to, nay love, those who can do what we can do ... only so much faster, higher, better. Ye olde gene pool calls for a dip each time the fluke's extra-ordinary performance sends shivers down our spine.

THE CELL-PHONE

"Reach Out. Reach Out and
Touch Someone"
(Slogan of Bell Telephone 1970s
to '80s)

Touch, touch! Pick, pick! Chatter, chatter! Watch monkey-behaviour footage and understand in a flash why the cell-phone has so rapidly conquered the globe. When humans conduct sociable sessions sending and receiving voice signals, they loll about, grimace, stretch, chew, yawn. At the same time hands are busy picking teeth, nose, ear, twirling hair, adjusting clothes, scratching here and there, drumming fingers, inspecting toes. Very simian! Even when the phone was still tethered to the wall, its triumph was based on ingrained habits from our evolutionary past. Ma Bell told us "to reach out and touch someone". We were convinced before we had to be persuaded because the slogan pushed some deep-time memory buttons. It's all about touching. Now that technology has freed us from the cord, we can talk-touch no matter when, no matter where, no matter the setting!

The following playlets from the stage of real life will show just how much we are wired to act as if a warm body were immediately attached to wherever there is a voice.

1. (1989) Having waited already for 3 ½ minutes to use the pay phone, I get a tad impatient and shift my weight to the other foot to indicate mild annoyance. *The look*

AHA! ✧ 31

comes my way from the booth. Another eternity, 1 minute and 23 seconds, passes. I emphatically shift again and sort of harrumph. The phone-using person, who has not uttered a word during those many minutes, **puts her hand over the mouthpiece**, turns to me and says: "I'm just listening to my messages."

2. (2000) I'm in the woods with a group of nature lovers. Somebody wants a bush break. During this forced down-time, one of those waiting on the path whips out his cell, dials, and stands there listening. Some old codger disapproves audibly. Mr. Cell **puts his hand over the mouthpiece**. Replies he, looking sternly at his critic, "I was just getting my messages at home."

Why cover the mouthpiece to listen to voices that come from a tape? Well, for eons to hear a voice meant that a living, breathing body was close by. So close that you might get a swat if you offended that body. The hand covers the receiver because the machine-voice is nevertheless a voice; it comes (so the synapses fire) from a sentient being, which being might be offended if we are rude enough to talk while he/she/it is talking![*]

The long-distance talking machine, carrying human voices that inform, threaten, caress, calm, entertain, has triumphed

---

[*] Conversely, when the voice is not there, we think no-body is there. Witness the embarrassing moments when TV anchors, commentators, politicians, corporate big cheeses have made utterances as if nobody (no body = no-ears) could hear them while the microphone or the speaker-phone were still "on" and listening!

world-wide to the saturation point because it lets us indulge in behaviour some 4 million-plus years old and by now hard-wired into our genes.* Apes are compelled to touch other apes constantly. If they're not just giving a quick pat, they run past each other with a quick jostle or flank-wave-tap. And a lot of touching goes on when *this* monkey de-louses *that* monkey while fingers comb along every inch of body through every tuft of fur. And listening to them is not unlike listening to the excited babble on stock markets, the din of voices in crowded malls, or the natter-chatter of a bunch of school kids standing at a bus stop, tourists emerging from a bus, or audiences before the beginning of a show.

The grooming & monkey-chatter has not evaporated over those millions of millennia while humans evolved from the apes. The need to groom is with us in our need to touch and be touched; our endless capacity for small-talk is the equivalent of the chatter that goes with the grooming. Until the omnipresence of the telephone in the middle of the 20th century, feeling close and feeling good came from chitchat within the extended family, the gossipy encounter in the village, and the proximity in living quarters so much smaller than ours today.

While the tribal and village life has disappeared in the better-mousetrap part of the world, the need for that kind of

---

* The astonishing growth in techno-prattle-hungry folk globe-wide is threatening our birthright to the seven-digit phone number. Is our pre-high-tech neurological brain up to storing several 10-digit or 12-digit numbers? But, hey!, we will get memory buttons to push just for prefixes!

behaviour and its good-feeling by-product hasn't disappeared. The hand-held speaking & listening device insinuates itself into our very core. Humans want to touch and be touched in return <u>and</u> chat at the same time. That's why the cell-phone is the colossal technological triumph it is. It fits an invented device to a natural inclination with absolute perfection. Something like it shall not pass this way again soon.

The urge to make grooming motions, that is combing with fingers through fur with rapid, repetitive motions, is with us still. That need to keep our fingers moving constantly has merely been transposed from rifling through fur to trifling with whatever happens to be handy. Anyone while on the phone and within arm's length of an office desk has made paperclip chains. Rare is the person who has not broken a toothpick into eight or more pieces while chatting on Alexander Bell's invention. All of us have, during this or that exchange of piffle, shredded a piece of paper or tissue into far too many pieces. The doodlers of unintelligible curlicues are legion. We shall draw a veil discreetly over those whose fingers do things with their scalp, patches of exposed skin, and that other ear not glued to the instrument.

The cell-phone, as was the case with the wall-tethered phone, has not made humans better conversationalists; it has, however, increased what's called "capacity". It has vastly increased the capacity for allowing yet more physical activity while we chat. Body parts we had to hold still while using the wire-cord phone can now move. We can roam while we talk. Although ostensibly designed, developed, marketed to put another arrow in the quiver of the deal-pursuing business person, the cell-phone rested only for a moment exclusively in that domain. Within the shortest of times it multiplied and nested in hands across the spectrum of human diversity and habitat. Now we can indulge in our primordial need for grooming and chatting, all the while doing modern things like crossing the street, steering the car, checking out stuff in a store, eating restaurant lunch with or without someone else, riding a bike, or being delayed in an airport.

A consumer item becomes part of the human environment only if it blends easily into the genetic behavioural landscape. The cell-phone fits our need for uttering sounds as well as our compulsion to try anything new. Our addiction to doodad-ism is the second reason why those handy[*] chatter-enablers fly out the electronic gear stores. The conviction which arises in us that we absolutely must have the newest gizmo is, aha!, based on excellent survival behaviour. Eons ago it helped one's DNA to become a link in the chain that extended beyond oneself. Satisfying the craving for the newest gizmo ensured first the invention and then the use of better tools with which to hunt, fight the enemy, build shelter, clothe children, prevent food from spoiling.

---

[*] The Germans call the cell-phone "Handy", a word which does now, but did not before, exist in their language.

The Cell-Phone

" ... wireless phones are the fastest-growing consumer product **in history** [emphasis mine], with about nine million now used by Canadians on a daily basis."

Times Colonist, 2001.03.08.

The invention of the cell-phone saves us also from a feeling we have tried to avoid since Day One, that of being bereft of human company, alone, deserted. As the invention and the spread of the motor car saved us from having to deal with the gigantic problem of horse-apple disposal in the wake of an ever expanding demand & supply for/of urban transit, so the invention of the cell-phone saved us, just in time, from an ever more serious collective case of isolationitis.

We sure miss the tribe of about 80 fellow creatures amongst whom to move and chat in close proximity. Learned tomes and pop-psych-paperbacks about our alienation from one another and the resulting angst stretch from the earth to the moon. Occasionally we feel the need to "do something about this" and somehow the wisdom of the folk concocts a nostrum. One such panacea managed to condense parenting advice from hundreds of books into a six word bumper sticker: "Have you hugged your kid today?" What would someone, freshly alighted from Mars, infer from this reminder? Presumably the being from Mars would know that we are wired for life in a tribe, at most life in a small village, but that we've voluntarily come to live among the anonymous multitudes of the city.

This public admission that the—evidently desirable but shriveled—monkey love needed to be plumped up and made to grow was followed by a decade and a half of obsessive concern with touching & feeling of, by, and for everyone. Self-help books, seminars, talk-shows, work-shops, therapists, daily newspaper wisdom proliferated because they tapped into our deep need for human contact and our equally deep unease with the harried, hurried, hyper-ventilating life which leaves neither time nor established conventions for touching on a frequent basis. We were told to touch each other, to hold each other, to hug each other, to get in touch with our feelings, to get in touch with our own truths, to communicate, communicate, communicate with all and sundry we encounter.

But soon anyone not wearing rose-coloured glasses could see that the goal to "get in touch with ..." remained obscured by a kind of diaphanous mist that never did allow clear focussing. All that babble about touching hadn't really made us into touchers after all. As it happened, during that same time new devices to serve communication, the fax and the pager, took hold in a serious way. Both were easy to use, both involved only a bit of fiddling, both made it easier to let that what we had to say (or wanted to hear) leap over great distances. The cell phone was not far behind.[*] Those gainfully employed persons who get the newest high-tech gadgets via the requisition sheet could now be seen using a cell-phone. By the time this particular accessory

---

[*] The appearance of new tools has speeded up a bit. The time span between the invention of the throwing spear and that of the sewing needle was roughly 2,000 years!

The Cell-Phone

materialized into every 11th hand*, the expression "circle of friends" had given way to "network". To say that so-and-so is good at "networking" has become praise equivalent to that bestowed in earlier times upon the churner of the smoothest, sweetest butter in the county. As the comparison to butter-making shows, networking (verb) is for women. For them it's a process; they establish relationships. Men enter a network (noun) of good ol' boys; they deal within the finished thing. I digress.

When all is said and done about the attempt to make every person have a passel of really close contacts, we're back where we started. The naturally gregarious creatures among us have the same enormous number of friends as they always tend to have; those more shy understand what "networking" is but not how to establish the nodes, never mind connecting them all. What almost everyone is good at, however, is plain old inconsequential but feeling-in-the-loop type chit-chat.

The cell-phone taking root in our hand saved us from emotional wilt. While fairly clunky in its early days, the goal to have it fit the size of our palm was reached within nano-seconds (measured on the scale of our 3 billion year evolution from the first "cell" capable of division and reproduction). The hand—albeit with the cell in it—once more becomes the instrument for touching those in our troupe. Separated by spaces too large to cross in one bound, bereft of ceremonial occasions which regularly make us rub shoulders, we move our fingers and touch—though without

---

* at the time of writing, in the United States alone over 160 million cell-phones are in use.

the body language or tactile satisfaction—another member of our tribe!

Which brings us once more to the tribe which anthropologists study, the kind within which we've spent 99% of our human evolutionary time. Being able to fit in and to express this fitting in by walking the walk and talking the talk like everybody else, ensured survival. All alone, without the tribe's collective knowledge, its support, its cooperation one quickly became a skeleton, a state not conducive to leaving one's DNA for replication. From birth to death a person would know familiarly between 30 and 150 other humans. Whether seeking shelter in a cave, in a primitive hut, or under the same large bush, contact with each other was close and very, very personal. "Huddling" in person-clumps created and conserved warmth. Sticking really close together discouraged attacks from animals or human foes. Ceremonies involved laying on of hands, braiding hair, painting each others' bodies. Children, from the baby to the toddler stage, were carried on hips, strapped to fronts and backs. And, since customary delousing survived well into the last century, one can make the assumption that this kind of touching contributed greatly to one's mental, as well as corporeal, health.

Homo sapiens has spent thousands of generations (about 40,000 years, or 2,000 generations ago, Cro-Magnon people displaced the Neanderthals) within a community of fellow beings who were all known by face, name, behaviour or, later, known at least as living in the same village or small town. Until only four generations ago, this was the environment in which almost everyone in the world functioned. Nothing has prepared our emotional nerve strands to cope with the anonymity in the crowded urban world.

No longer able to connect, as the monkeys do or the ur-human did, with fur and its lice, using our hands to grab, pull, pat, stroke, pet each other, we do that other monkey thing: we chatter. "Being touched" by a voice is deeply satisfying ... and it doesn't have to be the voice of Céline Dion, Placido Domingo, or Garth Brooks. We've all seen the interview with a rescued person emerging from long physical isolation caused by some accident or natural disaster. Invariably, they declare that the greatest deprivation was not being able to hear another human voice. The greatest punishment inside prisons is the isolation cell, the "solitary".

Although the key-pad is an integral part of the design of the phone, by happenstance it also fits how we have always tried to get someone's attention. Before we can reach out and touch someone, our fingers have to touch a bunch of buttons. By necessity we have to use our fingers to nudge and prod to attention the voice we want to hear. We can't get attention until we've used our hands. To use one's fingers to get someone to take notice of us, to be able to talk to them, precedes touching buttons by many millennia. From toddlerhood onward we tug on clothes, touch a hand, grab an arm to signal our need or willingness to talk. And often it's done even though the tugger has nothing much to say nor expects even a single pearl of wisdom. It is not the possibility that the connection might sparkle with brilliant discourse that sells a lot of cells! It is that we can establish on impulse that we matter to someone, be it ever so briefly.

Being able to chat at the moment the notion arises is such a seductive idea that maxing out the credit card is easily justified. The justification offered is that with the cell one can dial 911 on the spot. And this one, possibly life-saving, function of the device is trotted out every time a new cell possessor feels slightly defensive about the cost, the charges, or the irritant the thing may be to by-standers. Yet, not to put too fine a point on it, this thing may save a life here and there but it also goes the other way. An alarming number of people have been deprived of life or been brought close to losing it because their, or someone else's, hand, ear, attention were glued to that, yes, life-saving invention. It's the chatter that counts, not the crisp transmission of data. Chatter does not focus the mind.

What has brought us the cell-phone is what has brought us the hi-tech world. The evolution of our brain favoured the ability to think up and about what is **possible**. It did not develop to focus on what is **necessary**. The cell-phone is not a necessity. The human bio-mass increased to over 6.1 billion constituent parts without the cell-phone having been thought a prerequisite.

Consider the following vignettes and marvel how our ancient program, the need to chat, runs on the new hardware, the cell. Not a necessity in sight!

The mother/gatherer unit

Here she goes, pushing a shopping cart with one child inside it and one child hanging on. She is, to use the modern parlance, multi-tasking. With one hand—which also holds the shopping list—she pushes the cart; between her head and shoulder is wedged a cell-phone; her other hand grabs bags, cartons, bottles, chunks of this and bits of that. She is oblivious to the chirping of her young. Can there be any doubt that she suddenly felt an overwhelming need to do some chatting while gathering, something that her ancestors could do, and did for thousands of years, body within a few feet of another body whether collecting edibles in the Savannah or gleaning the remnants of the grain harvest. Since we weren't around then, we can't judge whether the children were as successfully ignored!

The alpha-male

We see him ride the biggest, showiest, most powerfully propelled horse of all time. It puts the rider into the conquering spirit. Basically, he's in hot pursuit of the aurochs, the bear, the deal, the trophy, the maneuvre that will enhance his status in the tribe. The empowering feeling of riding above the common herd has just been intensified. A tiny hand-held device allows this alpha-person to announce his importance long-distance. The chieftain of the firm no longer has to suffer the feeling of being of no consequence in that grid-locked mass of commuters. Press the speed-dial button and the feeling of importance, of, yesssss! power! floods your very veins. Give commands, ask to be informed, impose your presence.

The Cell-Phone

Just the same, what's lacking here, somehow, is the heroic dimension. Our mythic heroes had their wisdom shaped by silence and solitude. One spent 40 days and 40 nights in the wilderness to overpower temptation; another journeyed for years alone upon the back of a trusty (non-mechanical) steed to find the Holy Grail; a more recent one is the lonesome, tight-lipped cowboy full of salt-of-the-earth insights. Heck, even *The Terminator* would, at most, utter barely three words between pressing the on- and the off-button! It's safe to venture that our collective unconscious is not at ease with the picture of the alpha-male constantly flapping his lips.

The off-sprout

Whether roaming in motley collections of diverse numbers or dweebing alone at home, the young of the species have their own long-distance touching gadgets. All have a phone; many of them have cell-phones; lots of those who lack a cell have beepers. Using the beeper clicks into the same wiring as that of their adult kin: status is good; talking feels good; being connected to the tribe every moment of one's life is super-good. Technology has managed to assemble those three good!s at the touch of the button. Touch the button(s), touch a person, be touched in turn. Parents en masse are on record for feeling comfortable, reassured, good about having their teenaged off-spring within touching distance as it were, while slaving for the firm (and no longer on the farm).

This kind of touching with our voice suits us fine because it allows our contradictory impulses to co-habit. On the one hand, we like to be close, to hear that we're in the proximity of some other body. On the other, we do anything to establish our very own private and separately walled-off space, to get away from the herd. One side of us abhors silence when in the company of others, and we feel awkward when no one speaks. So we chatter and thereby touch. Then again, a room of their own has become a teenager's basic human right. The idea is to be alone, to get away from it all. Yet no sooner does the door close than the stereo, TV, or phone gets activated. Adults and seniors want to live independently which, mostly, means living by themselves. For them the TV set is on from early morning to late at night, often going full bore, to satisfy a nervous system that craves assurance that others of one's kind are close by.

For eons civilization has taken hold because its basic person unit has tried—and succeeded—to distance itself from close contact with anything. In the name of efficiency, of course. The broom distances us from rubbish; the plow from the dirt; the sword from having to strangle someone to death; the musket from having to swing that sword; the missile allows us to be yet more distant from contact with the body we want to kill; we move away from our tribe to cover the earth; we move from the city to the suburb; we drive the car to get away from it all. Way back when we evolved, it benefitted the tribal and individual DNA to strike out, to seek greener pastures, to start anew. That wiring certainly took hold because it worked so well for the survival of the species. That's us and we might as well run with it!

We've got to love that technological mega-hit that lets us keep distances yet lets our voices bridge them easily. At the very moment when the country-side, with all its opportunities for having space of one's own, is emptying out because folk want to be in the crowded cities where the action is and where the jobs are, we feel more apart than ever and in need of a tug at another's jacket. We use the cell to pull at someone's frock to let them know that we exist, to get feedback that we're connected. Maybe the hero is a hero to us precisely because he is self-sufficient and not in visible need to affirm his existence at every turn by using the echoing chatter. For the rest of us, having a cell means never having to be afraid that others don't know how we are, where we are, that we are.

So, yes, reach out and touch ... voice-mail.

THE WEATHER

> "Grand day, isn't it?"
> "Yeah, we deserve it after all that rain!"
> "Looks like it's gonna hold, eh?"
> "Well, that's what the forecaster says, anyways."
>
> (Everyperson, ca. 35,000 BCE - 2001+ AD)

Weather talk is human's caulk; it fills the chinks in our disconnectedness. The weather has been the most fundamental influence on our survival during 99.99% of our time on planet earth. The state of the weather and what it might "do" meant comfort or suffering, having enough to eat or having to go hungry, life or death. That's why the topic of the weather and what it is like, what it has been like, and what it will be like has an intrinsic hold on us.

We're pretty certain that we no longer have much in common with those ancestors who thought that spirits were responsible for bringing wind, thunder, or hail, and that the sun and moon obeyed an entity which controlled their rising and setting. Yet daily we can observe pesky out-croppings from our pre-civilization mental landscape and perform rituals which are rooted there still. Today the technology of the integrated circuit chip links every hill and valley. The rain of weather-*information* falleth on the city and the country in equal measure. We are glad of our barrels full of weather lore because they hold plenty to dip into when we share a sociable occasion. Being sociable is what our weather prattle is all about. Our many daily miniconferences about the state of the elements is a ritual and, by observing it, we demonstrate to others and ourselves that we belong to the tribe.

Culture follows nature. During our deep-time, evolutionary, tribal past, we've had a lot more nature act upon us than culture. And so it came to pass that our justified *concern about* the weather turned into an abiding *interest in* the weather. It's a cultural given that everyone shares the great fascination with the state of the weather. It's an observable fact that we're easily riveted to any data covering weather: be it the temperature today, the precipitation tomorrow, or the barometric pressure a year ago. We don't like to hear the phrase "before records were kept" because it calls to our attention that there's a lot of weather we don't have information about. We even care what the weather is doing in outlying areas within a twenty-one mile radius of where we dwell, a few provinces away from us, in countries we will never visit. It seems that lasting, almost obsessive, interest in the state of the weather has been, is, and will come with every edition of the entity called "person".

Certainly the WEATHER as an *ur*-topic has not lost its grip on us in these electronic times. Big talk, small talk, fact, fiction, surmise about the weather goes in one phone and comes out of another, occupies quite a few lines in e-mail, is always, always remarked upon in chat rooms, can be found as a little scrawled note at the bottom of faxes, is hunted on the Internet, appears as animated rain drops or sun rays on web-sites, can be viewed 24/7 on dedicated TV channels. The

The Weather

weather forms the largest single common topic in casual as well as purposeful human gatherings of two or more.

We care deeply about the state of the weather because every humanoid comes equipped with a sort of factory setting which pulses most reliably when activated by a weather-word. This setting keeps us absorbed in myriad details about atmospheric conditions and puts us in a state of fascination which gives us pleasure. If this weren't so, the more absurd outcroppings of this coding from ancient times—such as making the weather during a G-8 conference or an in-door convention of dentists an evening news item—would have been dispensed with a long time ago. Does it matter in Duluth, Minnesota whether the conference trippers in Miami, Florida need umbrellas or sun-screen? Save for a hurricane or blizzard, what kind of weather happens while the big *fromages* meet is irrelevant. These conferences take place indoors, deal with matters unaffected by the weather on the day of the agenda, are attended by men in suits and women in wearage sufficient to shield them from any probable barometric whimsy, and offer to the attendees and observers transportation in climate-controlled conveyances.

Excepting disasters, we live at a moment when the state of the weather no longer affects our survival. Yet we talk, read, worry about a fact of life which simply **is**. To this day we have no control over the weather. To this day the prediction of what the weather will be is still hit and miss, with an awful lot of misses. It's a bit humbling to recognize that our cultural evolution, including our present hi-tech state,

The Weather

accounts for changes on the surface but has not made a scratch in the sub-structure of where we come from.

Most of our globe's occupants live in cities, get their food from a store, can illuminate their dwellings around the clock, locomote protected by their own four-wheeled carapace, visit loved & liked ones by telephone, stray afield by television, have heat sources other than the sun or an open fire, and wear clothes which require neither killing a furry animal nor are difficult to replace and, not a small matter, dry ever so much more quickly than a pelt.

Of course, once upon that time long and not so long ago, the state of the weather influenced the success of the hunt and the gather. If it became too cold in the winter, freezing to death was an all too real possibility. Long periods of drought threatened to endanger the very survival of the tribe. Even if humans had enough to drink, neither the gather nor the hunt would yield much, certainly not enough to lay by a store for the long winter. Weather mattered.[*]

The elements mattered because they were directly responsible for the seven fat and the seven lean years during that relatively long period of our agricultural past. The elements mattered even more during that much longer time when the only creek nearby dried up, the lengthening of the days didn't bring the expected disappearance of the snow, a hurricane's devastation came unannounced—all without

---

[*] Those of our fellow earthlings whose daily nourishment still *does* depend on what the elements bring are paupers even in the possession of weather information.

pantries, super-markets, or international relief organizations. If any proof is needed that humans do not adjust their mental habits to a changed environment, even one so drastically changed as that in the industrialized, digitized, urbanized world in the last 150 years, consider the pre-historic grip the topic WEATHER has on us.

Why—if we spend our days and nights in homes where even the outhouse is inhouse—is our main topic of conversation a condition which

- cannot be reliably predicted
- only affects the quality of our lives in cases of meteorological irregularities
- is not a good candidate for being out-smarted by some technological invention?

Further, let's try to explain this template of behaviour, in up-dated permutations observable daily. During the 1970s, B.WWW (before world-wide-wiring and that other www.) a long-distance call to a party farther away than 100 miles qualified as an exciting break in the daily routine. Managers in smallish businesses used to make such calls not too often because they were expensive. Yet the boss, any boss, never ever, not once, made such a call without talking about the weather. If this stupefyingly mundane topic wasn't broached at the beginning of the conversation, it was sure to be the concluding number. At either end of the line the speaker could not do a thing about the weather there or here, suffered neither here nor there its consequences, nor ran a business that depended on the state of the weather. Yet these two industrial-age honchos were happy and fulfilled, definitely

The Weather

bonding over the *discussion*—if that's not stretching the meaning of that word—of a topic weighty only to the pre-historic hunter or the farmer.   Meanwhile the meter was running!

It's almost as if the WEATHER is not a topic of our conscious choosing.   Somehow this subject-matter arises unbidden from some deeply embedded circuit in our brains.   If we imagine the brains of this globe's entire population of 6.1 billion people as a kind of simmering porridge layer, we'd see bubbles arising randomly constantly, not a one exactly like another, but bubbles just the same, bubbles all over, bubbles all the time, bubbles the only activity. These bubbles are talk about the weather.   These bubbles let off the steam of human vexation.   Venting at each other citing specifics about family, job, or traffic would deplete our emotional resources; venting from the get-go about an unequivocally common experience replenishes our fellow feeling.   Venting about specifics carries with it the unspoken obligation to do something about whatever the grief; venting about the weather carries no such subterranean burden.[*]

The topic of the WEATHER pops up when two humans, sharing home and hearth, come to life over the first cup of coffee.   At the very least, "gonna be nice, eh?" or "did you hear the rain last night?" indicates that the dwellers are, if not much else, on speaking terms.   This opening gambit often leads to further ruminations about how the weather might be today, how it was yesterday, how its probable

---

[*] This very state of affairs makes Mark Twain's quip so timelessly funny: "Everybody talks about the weather, but nobody does anything about it."

The Weather

deportment might inconvenience or make perfect a scheduled event, and so on.

The topic of the WEATHER arises even among those who share a companionable activity in the great outdoors, right where everyone can not only see but feel the state of the elements. Thus it is that golfers or hikers or ball players share information known to every participant: how the weather was in the morning when they got up; what the forecast was in the paper, what the weatherman predicted last night on TV, how lucky they were to come out despite the threatened rain/storm/cold/fog/broiling heat; how surprised they were when they saw the clouds, the rain, the sun, the wind, whatever! change to ... etc., etc. Everyone, of course, lives in the same place, woke to the same weather, is seeing the same environment at that very moment. This is not an exchange of information; it's making the right noises to keep feeling good about being part of such a great bunch of fellow humans.

Fellow-feeling arises effortlessly when a thing or an idea can be shared. Sharing, however, presupposes that both, or all, parties care to share and know what they're sharing. It makes for a congregation of interest. What the high priests of goat-entrails prediction were to the ancients, the weather persons of the undulating satellite image are to us today. What happened in the temple then, happens in TV-land today. The enormous flock of weather-info-slurpers everywhere has lifted "the weatherman" to a station on par with, if not elevated above, the news anchor. A veritable personality cult grows, initially without backing by station or

The Weather

commerce, around the "meteorological specialist" (the new politically correct appellation). He/she receives letters, gifts, flowers, sent presumably in hopes that intercession with the weather-deity will thereby be granted a favourable outcome. As trusted friends and local celebrities, they congratulate those 100 years old or married for more than 60 years. They also promote communal events which lean toward making their particular weather-pocket a better place to live or the viewer a better person. At the point where they become the equivalent of one's favourite relative, they tend to branch out into doing commercials and making public appearances.

Talk about the WEATHER is the oil that lubricates social intercourse between neighbours and the folks up and down the street. The opening routine that it's a "nice day today, isn't it?" sets the right tone for imparting the news that there will be a birthday party with lots of cars and noise this night. In front of your house, you meet a woman you know by sight. You still don't know her name after living in the neighbourhood for three years. You do know that she lives in the pale green house and that she has a cat. Yet, the exchange of a couple of sentences about the relative quality of the temperature creates that warm feeling of being one of the block (tribe), of being close, of knowing, or at least getting to know, each other.

The Weather

This chapter is becoming as (seemingly) endless and as repetitive as the talk about the weather. But it's such a congenial topic! We never tire of "hot 'nough for ya?" or "lovely weather we're having". Will weather talk ever become boring? To find out, read on …

At work the topic of the WEATHER occupies salaried employees as much as share-optioned CEOs. "The weather" is the first thing to be mentioned in the morning, definitely remarked upon before going for lunch, deserves comment after returning from lunch, is surely brought up before leaving the office. Not taken into account here are the countless sentences uttered during the working day—on the phone, in the hall, in the washroom, in the cafeteria, at the copy machine, at the coffee machine, in front of and in the elevator—regarding the state of the sun, wind, rain, temperature, brightness, gloominess, forecast, weekend possibilities of **THE WEATHER!**

Occupying, as it does, many of our waking minutes, the WEATHER and all that this topic encompasses has become a veritable industry. Never mind that 81%+ of the world's people live in cities and under circumstances which make the state of the weather most days of the year irrelevant at best and an inconvenience at worst. One of the most successful and biggest industries is prospering because it supplies not what is *necessary* but what is *possible*. Next to the topic of sex, weather data clicks into the most visceral and ancient mechanism that makes us tick.

The Weather

Everywhere we're offered a multitude of choices in matters WEATHER. So intensely do we crave "news" about air and sky that no one has gone broke supplying any of the following:

- the money-making publication of the *Farmer's Almanac* (for all of us urban, suburban backyard, balcony, window-sill agriculturists!)
- the 10+ minute weather presentation on the nightly news
- the three minute weather up-date on radio and TV every hour on the hour
- the temperature read-out on tall buildings,
- the more than half-page coloured weather map in every newspapers edition
- the detailed pictographic reportage of the weather in places too far away to reach within a day's travel, also in the newspaper and on cable channels and on the Internet
- the thumb-nail weather graphic on the front page of every newspaper
- the predictable inclusion of drought, storm, hail, flood, heat-wave, cold-snap stories, local & distant, in the daily and in the nightly newscast
- the no-charge weather number in the yellow pages (financed by ads)
- the viability of cable channels exclusively devoted to 24/7 weather reports from around the world
- the existence of a HTML-link to a weather up-date on the home page of every popular search engine!

The Weather

- the vast armada of weather-forecast-gathering meteorological paraphernalia, the largest of which are land stations, ships, and satellites
- a movie in which the main character is a storm.

To add a zinger to this list, here's a thought-provoking item from May, 1999 (CBC, *Undercurrents*). It concerned what's sometimes called "storm porn", footage of unbelievable violence done by the WEATHER. Should you possess a camcorder and be in the right spot at the right time to shoot "severe weather", you've gotten close to money pots. The going rate (in 1999) was $56 per second of useable images! The appeal to the viewer(s) is that ages old, not quite conscious, response of "there but for the grace of God go I" coupled with the voyeur in us. Both make us want to be right there when untoward things might happen or do happen to one or more of our fellow beings.[*] Enough channels are big-time bidders for this kind of footage to infer that we are a long way from being as rational as we believe ourselves to be.

In that same neighbourhood of gather-hunter behaviour lives our comfort with, even need for, ritual. Quite a few connections from our need-for-ritual grid are wired into a compulsion-to-gather-weather-lore circuit board. Weather fixation seems to follow certain prescribed moves, moves within the same content basics. It certainly has its own

---

[*] Into this category falls the impulse to want to drive to see a building burn, a possible suicide, the scheduled imploding of a structure. (We want to be right there and look. To hear about a weather disaster from an eye-witness is ok. To read an unillustrated article about it is lame.)

ritualistic phrases. Rituals, by their very nature, follow a script that is so internalized that its performance seems a spur-of-the-moment thing. Partaking in a ritual in a given culture requires enough mental effort to be rewarding and little enough to enable just about everyone to participate.

Everyone can participate in ritualistic chatter which is, thank the gods, socially inoffensive, yet sufficiently potent to grease the workings of our casual-contact mechanism to create that good feeling of fellowship. Every time we chitchat about the WEATHER we partake in a kind of conjuring ceremony. Ceremonies bind us together. They make us feel part of something larger: our tribe, our surroundings, the cosmos.

THE FIRE & THE TALE

> Cross-Patch,
> Draw the latch,
> Sit by the fire and spin.
>> Nursery Rhyme

Nothing should surprise us about the rainbow-like arching success of television all over the world. Only one half century after the first broadcast in living colour, the glowing screen is an integral part of dwellings in the furthest reaches and tiniest niches of every culture on this globe. To us the television set is as essential as was the fire pit to our forebears in their shelter because the flicker and steady sound from the lit screen happens to snap right onto the grid of our species' experience with burning logs, peat, or dung. For tens, nay, hundreds of thousands of years we'd sit around a fire—most often during or after a good meal—and listen to someone telling a story. Our brains made the pictures to go with the narrative. Television is the success it is because it saves us the hassle: the "narrative" comes in pictures, created for us in living colour and available 24/7. And looking at pictures is—if that's not overdoing the computer analogy—our default setting. Merely looking entertains, soothes, informs, reflects old and makes new myths.

In the billion years of evolution from single cell to sentient being, the eye came first. Looking came long before hearing and talking. We're gawkers! That's what we do the most and like doing the best. The invention of linear print and the teaching of reading have not changed our predilection for the live picture one iota. Eighteen generations after Gutenberg and Caxton, reading the newspaper is only the #4 choice for "getting the picture" of what's going on. Radio is #3, while television is in the #2 spot for finding out what an event looked like. Being at the scene is #1 for checking out what's happening[*], if we get the opportunity. The technology of the rapidly moving pixels, second best to real-life gawking, triumphed over the technology of type-set print within only two generations—and it wasn't much of a contest!

We're hard-wired to love the open flame contained within some banked material. Which makes us "moderns" feel good around a fire: the burning logs in the chimney, the glowing coals on the barbecue, the sparking sticks for the marshmallow roast. Laws had to be passed against burning trash in one's yard; the impulse to set fire to rubbish goes back a while longer than remembering to take out the garbage for municipal collection. We've spent, at most, three generations with pipes or wires which bring to us heat for cooking or warming the body. Those genetic bits which respond to, crave even, a flickering flame have not had time to atrophy or be modified. We pay extra for the centrally heated house if it has a "real" fireplace. Heck, we even pay

---

[*] If you have any doubts, drive to the scene of a train accident, a spectacular fire, a person sitting on a bridge girder. Although warned by radio to stay away, although able to see "it" on the evening news, although not needed to help, the place will be traffic-gridlocked and human-stuffed! We act as if we still lived in a village and this were one's life-time defining event. Future generations will be telling tales about it. We might be able to chime in "I was there; I saw it with my own eyes!"

extra if it has an electric fireplace! That flickering tells our brain to expect feeling part of the tribe, safety, warmth, survival.

We haven't changed; our brains haven't changed; our responses haven't changed. But technology has changed. Electricity and hi-tech have presented us with a central hearth ready at the touch of a button. It's bright; it flickers; it makes noises. It's the TV, an electronic-age commercial success without equal. The same neural pathways that led to feeling good in prehistoric times today serve to soothe frayed nerves when the eye gets a glimpse of that flat screen with its dancing lights on it. It's that very old fire but a fire without the fuss and bother of first layering the kindling, getting the flame to bite, adding firewood, getting rid of the ashes last, and much stoking in between. TV is that very old fire and it has built in fireside-chats.

No matter where on our globe, ever since the 1950s a television was a must-have for family or singleton. Universally the appeal is on and to the level of the human species' nervous system, and it does not seem to depend on the culture in which that system lives. That squarish thing with the moving images on it works for us because it requires no more effort than would sitting and "scanning" a fire. The screen manages to project a bunch of pixels, little coloured dots, which the eye first scans, then sends to the brain, and that marvel of evolution makes a picture out of the dots. Since the invention of fire, sitting and imbibing pixels has made us feel snug. Imbibing various snack items has been part of that most congenial, warming, entertaining pastime for eons as well

Way back when, long before our Cro-Magnon past even[*], we started getting coded to associate the flickering flame with creature comforts and survival itself. As the glow of fire triggered feelings of well-being then, so the electronic blaze of bright pixels provides succor for our harried souls today. Like no other invention, the fire's flames integrated the physical with the spiritual, the warming of the body with the warming of the soul. Watching the movie *Quest for Fire*, we root for those three brave, inventive, enduring fire seekers. They ensure the tribe's survival. Their progeny live; they're us. Fire is our ur-element.[†]

It was the need for warmth and light that gathered the tribe around the fire. And while sitting there and talking and listening, in time a gathering brought forth the telling of tales. The tales, accompanied by gestures and re-enactment, entertained the audience with the adventures of the hunters.

---

[*] People who study this sort of thing are now pretty well agreed that the invention of fire dates to between 800,000 years to 1.2 million ... that's a lot of coloured "flicker" watching! Give or take a few, 50,000 generations of us have lived lives with the fire as the central must-have of daily existence.

[†] As if proof were needed! During the Christmas holidays of 1999 a community channel in Victoria, BC, showed nothing but a 6-hour loop of a 2-hour real fireplace fire. No commercials, no station breaks, no logo. The fire was mesmerizing. It soothed the urban soul to watch the flames and sparks, to listen to the real-audio crackle and pop, to see the log being consumed, the fire occasionally stoked, then a log added. This "show" proved immensely popular, was briefly resurrected to allow people to tape it, and is now for sale on video cassette!

The Fire & the Tale

No doubt the wisdom of the elders would also be passed on and be more memorable for being offered in that setting. Whether song, some kind of rhyme, or dress-up-acting, the ground was being prepared for our fondness to be entertained first and to learn, if at all, secondarily.

Told by the open fire and over time, good stories repeated often became myths. These explained the world, assigned the human a place in it, and gave meaning to life. Though not a real fire, television's flickering accompanies the telling of tales. On that glowing square in the semi-darkness of our private spaces those tales are still about what can happen, what does happen, what to do, how to do it, funny stuff, sad events. Whether fire-tales or TV-series, a lot of the content is make-believe of the most outlandish sort. The difference is that our ancestors had to use imagination and call upon a hoard of words to "show" exceptional mortals living through amazing but exhilarating events, whereas today we call on the special FX studio. The knight who slew the dragon has become robocop. The underlying narrative hasn't changed though.

What may have changed—one guesses!—is that neither cave nor village performances were interrupted by messages about the new and improved herb-gathering basket Mrs. Cave-Bear had devised or the high-torque tolerant grinding stones the miller had acquired "so as to be better able" to grind flour superior to that of the competition. All else was the same. Fire was a necessity for any group of *Homo,* from *habilis* to *sapiens sapiens.* In much the same way, TV today is a necessity and not a frill. The glimmering narrative occupies "down" time, fills the lonely day of the old and sick, provides fodder for café-latte talk, baby-sits, offers something entertaining for almost everyone on the globe, mirrors as well as creates fads, socializes the young, pegs us in the scheme of things, provides our myths. And we find out what's new! So did the Cro-Magnonite tribe, assembled by the communal fire, from the mouth of the chief, the elder, or the shaman.

It's our most long-standing relationship, those fires and us. Not only do we love the fire; over time it has changed us. The thought processes and tasks necessary to produce, control, and maintain fire happened initially under certain conditions in a specific environment. After two or three thousand generations (which occupy between 40-60,000 years) the behaviour pattern necessary to have and maintain a fire must have become hard-wired.

To keep a fire going demanded foresight and planning; it wanted thinking that is not completely concerned with the present and immediate gratification. To begin with, those upright walkers had to find or know how to start a

Behaviour is adaptive. Non-random selection will see to it that survival-enhancing adaptation will become genetically encoded. Population-wide encoding takes eons = between 500 and 1,000+ generations, which means between 15,000 to 25,000 years. To put that in perspective: it's only been 100 generations since the birth of Christ.

fire. Then they had to keep the flame alive. They had to learn to plan and carry out the plan: collect and stack enough fuel to feed the fire; if the stack gets low, go out to find more fuel; keep the supply dry; with the cold season approaching, gather lots of wood or dung or peat; prepare it and store it. And never, ever leave the fire alone for more than a few hours. Those tribes who as a matter of course, day after day, had flames for warmth, for cooking, for frightening away dangerous animals survived ... and are our far-off ancestors. It's doubtful that we can find DNA today of those who couldn't get their fire-act together![*]

Thousands of years followed, all the while the fire was central to the cave, the tent, the longhouse, the yurt, the hovel, the dug-out, the farm kitchen, the city dweller's fine mansion. Manor houses were judged by the number of fireplaces they contained. Almost all entertainment—from sing-song to playing charades, reading aloud, telling stories, visiting with neighbours, whittling or stitching—took place where the fire burned and warmed. That's why our nervous system gets all gooey when it comes close to a fireplace-type fire or a reasonable facsimile of it.

Television, a most reasonable facsimile, spread with, well, the speed of a wildfire. It penetrated first into every dwelling in those countries that had, by and large, flame-less central heating. Its conquest of every household is not the result of the invention of merely another entertaining toy. Television flourishes in the niche left vacant by the departed open fire. This "new and improved" fire is ever so much

---

[*] Actually, maybe that was the first goal-oriented behaviour of our species: want something specific; plan how to get it; labour toward the result; labour some more to keep what you achieved; feel satisfaction.

more entertaining to watch than a bunch of flames or dying embers. This one comes with moving pictures and requires neither gathering of wood nor boot-blacking of the hearth. And sheer delight! a different story as well as story-teller can be had every time we turn a knob or press a button on the remote. We're new-stuff maniacs. In evolutionary times it was a survival value to give in to the temptation to try anything not experienced before. After all, the attempt to try something new can have only three outcomes: it kills you and it's the end of your DNA; it does nothing and you've had some excitement; it helps you survive better and longer and you get and keep more of your DNA out there.

What our "new-stuff = survival-value" program has not built in is an intuitively accessible, large-capacity sub-routine for the discernment of quality, that is, complexity. Throughout the ages, high-minded humans amongst us cherished the dream that if only complex and/or educational entertainment could be cast broadly among the viewing public, that public would gratefully choose to find edification entertaining. No such luck.

Technology offered universal access to the most beautiful and most stimulating works that human creativity had ever fashioned. But the appeal of TV programming showed quite a different curve, one much shaped like a horseshoe standing on its two ends. First, during the new-fangled invention phase, sitting or standing a few feet from the thing, one was riveted to what appeared on the screen.[*] "Oh, they're home, watching the test pattern" became a standing joke. Then the

---

[*] ... even in the rain, in front of a store window displaying TV sets!

curve went up steeply with theatre, opera, concerts, lectures, talking heads, documentaries, in-depth commentaries available in almost all time-slots. The medium still being more fascinating than the message, the curve flattened only a bit, but then descended. We, the people, endowed more popular fare—what became pop-culture—with robust ratings.

The $64,000 question was answered: entertainment beats education any time. Amusement, the fire fix, was no longer restricted to the late or dark winter hour; images soon could be summoned anytime, night or day. When the clickie—also known as *the remote*—fell from the high-tech fairy's hands into ours, it clicked (what else?) into our human programming while allowing us to click into the programming on the tube. It lets us hunt for the less booooring program; it lets us gather the gist of two or three ball games during one half hour. We may have our butts glued to the couch but our neurology loves roaming; we love the new, change for change's sake.

Which roaming has brought us back to pattern-watching. In the cable universe, we click ourselves from channel to channel; we "surf" on the ocean of patterns; we try to catch the wave. Nothing has to be related by story line or imagery, argument or reason; what matters is the change in patterns. Although women clickie-speedsters are known to exist, by and large the gatherers are out-classed and out-maneuvered by the hunters. The more images you can scan on the horizon, the more plentiful the potential kill. For the male,

The Fire & the Tale

TV is the fire against which he seeks to re-enact the hunt or have it re-enacted for him.

Not all is gathering and hunting, however. Occasionally the human must have a break in the routine. Enter the holiday or Holy Day. We intuit that these "destination" days must have existed from the time that we could put thought to thought and eventually remember a chain of thoughts. This is why one cannot discuss our sacred fire-box without dwelling for a moment upon the other kind of TV use: "designation watching".

Much like "designation gambling", the nature of the beast is not altered by having it singled out, decorated, and ritually fed. Thus it is that the screen is being lit at an ordained hour to have certain rituals enacted which will give us that comfortable feeling of becoming integrated with something larger than our little selves. Providing a kind of ceremonial orderliness in our increasingly chaotic world falls to the ministrations of the "designated broadcast". For it we invite friends, prepare special snacks, procure carbonated drinks, snuggle into comfortable upholstery, place the eats within arm's reach, and turn the floor lamp down a few watts. We're ready to have some ancient strings plucked and we relax deeply. The magic performance begins.

In the hierarchy of broadcast ceremonies, the **sports event** is emperor of the world. Its appeal does not depend on the language one speaks, the education one has, or a specific cultural context. In this event, an easily counted number of performers concerns itself with only one objective. Either a fixed number of them, fleet of foot, strong of arm, and fit of figure, try to propel an object accurately to some stipulated point. Or one single athlete tries to triumph over others more or less like him by propelling himself/herself faster, higher, over a longer distance. A hallowed set of rules has to be obeyed under the watchful eye of a judging entity. The spectators participate vicariously in victory or defeat. Nothing here suggests that we've become more complex beings since that very first "hit-that-stump" stone-pitching or "who'll be first to touch the menhir yonder" running contest.

Next in the hierarchy is the **glitterati-celebrity event**. It rules as king for those who live with electricity, television sets, and have access to Hollywood's products. The yearly Oscars are watched by over 100 million people all over the world, in something like 140 countries. Those who entertain us are admired, commented on, and taken as role models much as chieftains, kings, saints were in former times. The Hollywood A-list, acknowledged without protest by us nominally democracy-loving creatures, is our royalty. We pay homage by rendering the studios the wherewithal to make out paycheques to the reigning personages for $20 million+ per movie. We pay obeisance; we blink not at ancestral privilege. Today we tender levy to the second and third generation of actors who were literally "to the screen born". That's how hereditary "betters" come into being. We line up our bottoms on the couch to watch the crowning of the top five nobles of the screen much as our ancestors lined the thoroughfare along which the king's coach was rumoured to come travelling.

The Fire & the Tale

Third is **the real-time, real-life drama**, relatively new to TV but as old as the hills to our wiring. Its audience is limited to those who speak the language of the country in which the saga unfolds. Whether the O.J. Simpson trial, Princess Diana's funeral, or the Bill & Monica & Starr-show[*], the event unfolds moment by moment while we are actually "there". This equivalent of being at or running to the scene of the excitement-causing episode is precisely what happened in cave-days, in the early settlement, or in the medieval town. This "show" is tailor-made for what our brains are still the most comfortable with, minutiae. It's the tale, the drama, unfolding by the minute and by the day, about human beings we get to know and, therefore, think we know. As soon as we think we know the players, we have something to gossip about, and delicious gossip binds members of a tribe together.

The TV real-life serial also taps into another useful evolutionary gift: a picture can replace 1000 words; a picture cannot lie.[†] Before the printing press, all information—save what we heard but often did not believe—came from direct observation. Although we may know that a picture can be technologically modified, our ganglia are not quite up to sorting that out when we see hundreds of thousands of them in rapid succession. Our brain puts them together into what we're familiar with, what we don't care to examine. OJ's predicament becomes the tale about high life, hot temper,

---

[*] Although these are famous examples from US broadcasting, Canada had its wall-to-wall coverage when former Prime Minister Trudeau died.
[†] This may change as we all become wise in the ways of digitally altering an analog photographic record.

how the great have fallen; Diana's every move fed our archetypal princess image: youth, beauty, charitable deeds; Bill & Monica embodied the titillation of the bodice-ripper while reminding us that "Thou shalt not commit adultery". Letting us see all those pictures upon pictures of the (momentarily) exalted feeds into another predisposition of ours: we cherish the "warts and all" of the reportage; it allows that identification process without which a tale does not survive, a parable does not nest, ratings feed at the bottom.

Speaking of feeding ... during that grand entertainment—whether reclining on animal skin or couch—we do enjoy our watching experience more when in the company of kindred or buddy folk, bowls of chips, bottles of pop, cans of beer. Munching and swigging are as important as commenting on the action. Food-stuffs to watch TV by are chosen according to some left-over code bits from 800,000+ years ago when the nibbling was done around the fire. We tend toward:

- fat-laden, crunchy, salty chewables, the pre-historic survival food: fat plus that most precious of commodities, salt;
- sugared, flavoured drinks, once a rare treat made from what summer berries and rarely found honey could be spared;
- beer, the descendant of fermented "anything" mash.

Eating and drinking goes with the kind of entertainment that makes, as the saying has it, even "medicine go down". Most of this modern teller's tales are offered as distraction, light amusement, the horse race kind of thing. So it is that chomping on food and gulping drinks is not tolerated during church service, a theatre performance, or in the concert hall. Having to digest munchies makes the body re-route blood from the brain to the stomach. World-wide success comes to that kind of entertainment which does not require that the brain pulse with lots of the red stuff. And where the ratings go, there goes the programming. Hello! infotainment.

The story telling sage of yore had, no doubt, a sonorous voice, a commanding presence, and a facility with gestures. He's morphed into our self-possessed anchor person[*] who presents the Truths of our time reassuringly. An added comfort factor is that—whether delightful or horrible— today's tales are made easy on the emotions by having commercials break whatever tension may arise in the audience. After 50 years of the medium's existence, the narrative of the commercial has become often as compelling as the narrative of the main event. Never mind! Onward with telling tales. The "break" consists today of a succession of three (at least) disconnected mini-narratives about the merits of a certain beer, car model, pain reliever, hair enhancer, cereal, dog food, electoral candidate, cyber connection, garden tool and much else. A primordial yarn like *Baywatch*, with a primordially (therefore culture-neutral) shaped heroine, manages to peddle wares in almost 130 countries every day. A global success.

---

[*] An anchor may not be ugly—that's a law! #1: regular features do not detract from the message. #2: we believe good-looking people more readily than irregular-looking ones.

The Fire & the Tale

What we see, hear, understand in front of that pixel-fire shapes us because it reflects our culture. Nothing in that back and forth adjustment has changed from the day when a tribe learned who they were and how they should live while looking at a living fire and listening to tales. Today, in the global village, the tribe of the world looks at the same kind of show & tell. Soon, as it was in that far off time, a monoculture will hold sway. Our pre-historic brains will have no problem with that.

THE AUTOMOBILE

> A horse! a horse! my kingdom for a horse!
> William Shakespeare,
> *Richard III* [V, iv, 7]

So you think you're driving a car? You're doing no such thing! You're riding a bronco, or a cougar, or a wildebeest. You're taming the mustang so you can ride it and explore greener fields. This much is true of steed and automobile: you're faster than the footed crowd; you're wearing your own steel armour; you and the beast are more powerful than either one of you alone. And, as with riding a real honest-to-goodness animal, it's not always clear who is in charge.

But we like it that way. Humans like nothing better than a challenge. Give them a stone and they'll think up ways of how to make use of it, that is, make it do their bidding. Sometimes the stone wins! But if we win, we win by making a tool that works for us during our DNA-spreading life-time. Soon everyone wants to have and use the tool. No tool, no invention, no idea ever gets to be wildly successful with us unless it's connecting to behaviour that made our progeny survive from Day One. Our infatuation with the car is evidence enough of this. Its hold on our emotions, its profound impact on our behaviour, the toll it takes on our wallets has been seriously examined as well as made fun of. Even those who pay earnest attention to the various commentaries, studies, reports decrying the evils of our four-wheeled familiar get their car keys and drive what would take them 20 minutes to walk or 5 minutes to bike.

We may try to fight our sometimes surreptitious, sometimes palpable love affair with the car. But it's a fight we cannot win because by inventing the car, the ultimate fantasy of the first upright walker has been fulfilled: the wind, in the shape of a four-legged speedster animal, has been tamed. Now we can sit high above the savannah and fleet-footedly pursue the prey while riding above, in front of, and faster than the rest of the herd—animal or human. In the end it was not necessity but the flight of fancy that was the mother of this particular invention.

The first tamed animal serviceable for riding was the horse, of course. This goes back a few generations, about 250. Therefore, our abiding love affair with the car as a knock-off version of our ancient relationship with the equine is not only quite touching but also understandable. Some car vocabulary is still tied to horse. Every new technology borrows terms from the previous one. Computer terminology like "Desktop", "folder", [e]"mail", "wallpaper", "notepad" refers to words an office-slave during the reign of Queen Victoria would not have had trouble understanding. It's the same with car talk. We pull away from the curb, go for a ride, load the trunk. The power of a single horse is still the bench mark for measuring the output of our metal steed. After almost four generations with nary a living, working, prancing equine within our field of experience, we still ask the car dealer: "how many horses has she got?"

The Automobile

As we would have given a name to our horse, most of us give a name to our car. That we talk to, swear at, cajole our four-wheeled friends goes without saying. We do this in tones loud enough for that wordless helper to get the message. Many of us will admit that we pat or pound the dashboard while doing so. We tend our car almost as we would have a horse. Men particularly give their cars a good rub-down, using sudsy fluids, circular motions, and a high level of energy to bring that metal coating to a fine lustre. Women, whose relationship with the horse, presumably, was not as pervasive as that which men enjoyed, treat their cars as they do their dishes. If you have to, you can clean it by hand; if you can afford to, you take it to a mechanical wash; if you're lucky, the male(s) in your life will do the chore.

The "gitty-up-go" procedure involved before departing with a car shares similarities beyond the saddling of the horse; it links us to our most ancient ancestors. The reverie on the African veldt about controlling and riding a powerful animal has been turned into pulsating, exhilarating, empowering ecstasy at the turn of a key and a prod with the foot, both of which make the heap of metal roar. The mighty bellow warns every neighbour, bystander, or passer-by to get out of the way of the hunter and the brute that does his bidding!

Revving of a motor falls into that category of human actions which are at one and the same time done on purpose but not on purpose. Of course, pushing repeatedly the pedal to the metal has its justification: to warm up the engine; to get the fuel-line cleared; to get rid of condensation in the muffler. Whatever ... anyone who has complained about that racket with its foul exhaust-emitted stench has heard a litany of reasons why noise must first be generated before one can ride off. Right here belongs the observation that not one of the revvers fills their Day-Book with entries reading "fill immediate environment with noise and stench". These frustrated bronco tamers are, more often than not, law abiding citizens, good dads, willing handy persons around the house, salt of the earth employees. However, having inserted the key, (metaphorically speaking) they drift back in time. They come out of the cave, stomp around to warm up, grab the slingshot, snap it smartly against their thigh a few times, yell "rowowowaaarrrr!", and rush into the yonder to catch what they and their kin need to eat, to live, and to keep their DNA out there.

Every repository of that successful DNA—that's every car rider—gets into an invention that conforms to a very basic, unvarying design: four wheels, four sides, at least one window on each of those sides, solid bottom, solid top, front part that pulls, main part that carries the rider and the feed/fuel, butt part that contains whatever goods. Humans are not good at tolerating same old, same old. They love change. If change cannot be had, they tend to embellish such fixed shapes as their bodies, their clothes, their tools.

While we like to fit in, we also want to stand out. We're always trying to be different and special. That's why we choose, individually or as a group, clan totems, regimental colours, company logos, that special haircut, a lip stud, the family crest, baggy cargo pants, purple-silver nail polish. At the same time we want to fit in and be accepted by whatever tribe: hobby club, office folk, fellow clerks, professional colleagues, soccer moms. That's in sync with a left-over bit of coding that made us conform in ur-days so as not to be shunned or even cast out into the antediluvian wilderness by the disapproving members of one's band.

Humans need to combine standing out with fitting in goes into over-drive when presented with the chance to make distinct the object of their passionate attachment. We've all heard it said, maybe choose to believe, that it is the evil car makers who tempt us with "options", who needlessly bring out new models every year, who gizmo-ize basic mechanisms, who fix what wasn't broken. Yet the car makers could no more sell a single semi-customized car than a single wild horse could have been tamed if it didn't elicit enthusiastic responses in our waking hours from somewhere we know not! It so happens we tend to think in line with fantasies of the hunter and explorer of way, way a long time ago.

It's possible that our personal choice of a vehicle with its specific model-name does, indeed, identify us more than we think.

Companion:
Sidekick; Tracker; Prowler; Civic; Sprint; Accord; Integra

Status by the number:
Mercedes 360; BMW E5; Porsche 911; VolvoS90

Workhorse:
Tracker; Maxima; Pathfinder; Blazer; Sentra; Forerunner; Trooper; Explorer

Hunter &/or Totem:
Firebird; Cobra; Viper; Bronco; Ram; Impala; Mustang; Cougar; Jaguar; Raider; Windstar

In a league of its own is the [Ferrari] Testarossa for the red-blooded, testosterone-flooded alpha-male wanna-be.

The Automobile

The manufacturers of all those herds of self-propelled, domesticated stallions satisfy our compulsion to cherish the distinguishing feature by offering us the four-wheeler in shapes made possible by the steel press and colours concocted by modern chemistry. We can choose from designs as cute as a baby's cheeks and googly-eyes (the new beetle) or elegantly severe as that fluid line of the jaguar's body. We can pick a stream-lined shape vaguely reminiscent of boats, or carts, or earthly belongings sewn into a skin to be dragged behind an animal (the cube UTE). We may want to belong to the brotherhood of GM or the sisterhood of Volvo. What we do is make a statement about ourselves by choosing to belong to that particular 'hood. The nitty-gritty of what we desire, can afford, mean to show the world when it comes to the choice of "options" belongs into the realm of choosing to wear your hair short or long, to let the waistband of your underwear show or not, to carry a fanny-pack or a purse with handles.

The freedom of the road has to be matched by the freedom to choose from a bewildering smorgasbord of performance specs, shapes, colours, accessories, interior decorations, exterior trimmings, price tags. Predictably enough, once the novelty of small-unit horseless locomotion had worn off, the offer of "you can have this model in any colour as long as it's black" was no longer tolerable. Way back when, in leg-powered days, we tied a strip of leopard skin or a helical bone into our hair to show the singularity of our person. Many centuries later we wanted not only ourselves but also our horse-power individualized. Halter brasses, brilliant plumes to bob between the horse's ears, the blanket in the

The Automobile

colour of the owner's stable made one's equine team unique. Today that same impulse in the horse-power buying public encourages car makers to offer configurations of embellishments way beyond the necessary because we look for fancyfication when we go on the kicking-the-tire expedition.

Kicking the tire has taken the place of looking a horse, about to be purchased, in the mouth. Only in the case of the proverbial gift horse one didn't do the dental exam; even an old nag could do more and heavier work than one or two humans.[*] Which brings us to another deeply rooted appeal of that ubiquitous minion, the car. Since time immemorial status was associated with having slaves or servants. More status accrued if their number was sufficient to have them carry one about the place. This conveying hither and yon of the rich and powerful started, no doubt, with the tribal chief being transported on linked hands or on massed shoulders. From this evolved various kinds of litter contraptions, then anything that could be built and put on/above wheels and be pulled by humans or animals.

It's with us still, this thinking that being carried equals being the great one. Road rage, aggressive driving, absence of civility arise from the notion that, given that you are high enough in the pecking order, your ability to own transportation other than your legs shows that you have been favoured by the gods. Not only do you sit higher up, you

---

[*] Our equivalent of the much-used, and probably whipped, horse is the "beater" car. It's not clear whether this refers to previous or future "beatings" of the vehicle.

The Automobile

also lord it over others by doing so. Behind our automobile "coach" behaviour lurks the commoner's centuries-old pledge: one day! one day! when I have a horse, a coach, I'll show you!!

And so we come to wishes, dreams, aspirations expressed in folklore and myths. The navigable, self-propelled, accelerable, self-contained, plenty big enough sanctuary is an invention of the 20th century that managed to come as close to the illusion of effortless, distance-conquering, affordable travel as practicable. The car made real the scores of "stories" from our past. Myths give expression to that which we see as possible without having reality intrude upon the weaving of our imaginary life.

Our longing in the past to escape being tied to the earth, to the spot is, well, legendary. The giant with the seven-mile boots; Jack on his sky-ward growing beanstalk; Icarus whose wax wings melted when he got too close to the sun; Alexander the Great's beyond-horse Bucephalus; the Valkyries riding through the air; Pegasus, the flying horse; Mercury, a god with wings on his feet; angels, witches, dragons that take flight; every one of these mythic beings defied inertia or gravity. We'd still be somewhere in (what is today) Africa were it not for this longing to move, be on the move, and move again to a new beginning, to where the grass may be greener, to where we can be lord over our own cave, piece of land, domain. Move out; move away; move up! Our very selves are tied up with an assumption, however deeply hidden from our waking thoughts, that movement fast & far will make life better and bring happiness.

The Automobile

That which drove our species to leave our mark in every nook and cranny of the world drives us still. It's an illusion that we are in the driver's seat!

NOISE

> Beethoven's Fifth Symphony is the most sublime noise that has ever penetrated into the ear of man.
>
> E. M. Foster, *Howards End*

We're noise junkies and we need our daily fix! All kinds of sounds affect us in all kinds of ways: they give us pleasure; they reassure us that we're alive; they tell us that we're not alone. One and the same sound can be good-time music to some and intolerable noise to others. Then there is the loud noise instant buzz. Long, long ago a loud noise made one of our glands squirt adrenaline into our system to fuel either a fight or flight reaction. Obviously this was an evolutionary good. Shots of adrenaline coursing through our veins in the 21st century still give us that speedy onset of an exhilarating high-alert + totally-alive + shock-shiver state. Because that noise-"high" is innate to our pleasure-repository, it'll be a months of Sundays before we give up our auditory addiction.

Hunter-gatherer daylight times were accompanied by the low level noises of rudimentary activities. Humans talked, chipped stone, scraped hide, the brook babbled, birds sang, fire crackled. Those sounds made us feel comfortable, connected, safe. They also settled into our memory a connection between certain sounds and survival-ensuring activity. The thumping, trumpeting, snorting, inexorably advancing noise from an overpoweringly mighty animal would have been the more frightening for coming into such a quiet setting. Equally heart-pumping were horrible

Noise

screeches, clamor, and war whoops. They announced humans not of one's own tribe. Mostly they carried out their bad intentions, shouting and yelling amid the din made by those cowed. They raped the women, stole the fire, and maimed or killed whatever stood in their way. Nature's noises also portended no good. Neither early warning nor defense existed against the roaring forest fire, the howling storm, the crashing waves. Thunder claps frighten many of us today even though we know how they come about. Abject terror must have filled every single human during a thunderstorm in those far off days. Whatever the occasion, our forepersons had their blood pressure raised, their senses sharpened, and their bodies readied for action by sound waves many in numbers and high in decibles.

Nothing changed much when staying put and tilling the soil provided for daily life. In agricultural times almost everyone lived in a small community. Despite a somewhat larger population and human-built shelter, panic struck the heart of man, woman, and child upon hearing the awful whooshing, crackling, high-pitched ever coming-closer rush & rumble of a mighty storm. That noise announced that everything might get flattened, including the yet to be harvested grain. Human enemies, while setting dwellings on fire and generally trying to lay waste to the community's belongings, tended to shout, holler, and scream[*]. But every loud and unusual noise—made by a mad bull, bolting horse, or run-away cart—put the listener into high-alert mode.

---

[*] We get a remnant rush when listening to regimental bagpipers or shouting ourselves hoarse during sports events.

Noise

The soundscape we're still wired for today is the one in which we spent our everyday lives pretty well up to the 19th century. Judged by today's limitless possibilities of auditory output, pickings were slim and pretty dull. In really early ages singeing meat, splitting wood, chipping stone tools may have sounded comforting but rated low on the adrenaline meter. Equally unexciting was the daily noisescape in the farm world. It featured the human voice, the lowing coming from domestic animals, the clanking of yoke and harness, the crunching of wooden wheels on dirt roads, the hammering, banging, and ratcheting that came with life and work. The singing of birds, the rustling of leaves, or the soft whistling of the wind could be heard without ever being drowned out by the din caused by planes, trucks, combines, pile drivers, radios on max volume or any of the myriad penetrating stabs into aural quietude today. In village times one had to stand pretty well right next to the blacksmith whacking the horseshoe to flinch at a noise.

Just the same: standing there, wincing at every blow upon the red-hot iron, a body could observe that something pretty terrific was happening. The physical-assault strength noise and the making of useful, sometimes even beautiful, objects went together. Actually, many of the noises that barged into a relative quiet space meant that something or other was being prepared for comfort or survival: felling a tree; hammering together a dwelling; flailing during threshing of grain. And so another bit of content was added to our sensory memory banks: a connection between noise, activity, and the more pleasing life.

Noise

A not insignificant consideration, whether conscious or not, is the fact that those who make a noise are also known to exist. Making a noise broadcasts "hey!, I'm alive; I'd like somebody to take notice!" The farmyard works the same way: the cock crows to announce that he's ready for action; the hen cackles to advertise the production of an egg; a cow lets go of a certain moo when she wants milking. A cat can purr, hiss, meow, each sound announcing a different feline mood. Pigs snort and snuffle before, while, and after feeding, rooting, wallowing in mud. Even the bee's buzz advertises busyness.

Humans, who have bigger brains than bees and are endlessly inventive, add to the sounds coming from their bodies those cast about by their inventions. And as humans went forth, multiplied, and technologized, their arsenal of noise-emitters—and the volume to go with it—fructified in tandem. Noise supplies the daily adrenaline fix, serves as activity indicator, and confirms our existence. It does not, therefore, come as a surprise that nary a murmur arose to protest the ever increasing decibel level in the daily life of the burgeoning industrial age. Instead we seem to have welcomed—or tolerated as signals of progress a multitude of clangorous sounds: reverberating factory machinery, heaving steam engines, clattering chain-driven devices, the incessant commotion within tenement buildings, the clop-clop & wheel-rattle from the rapidly increasing hackney traffic before the invention of the internal combustion engine which, of course, brought its own onslaught of traffic noise.

Noise

The electronic age, making its entrance hard on the heels of industrialization, added all manner of technoidally generated as well as electronically amplified sounds. Along with bliss experienced upon listening to some sublime results from the mucking about with digital sound technology, we like or endure or ignore the banal emanations from woofering and tweetering speaker-boxes in elevators, malls, private offices, any kind of government bureaucratic warren, boutiques, supermarkets, even in loos. Gradually—if one can call "gradual" a mere generation's time-span of 20 years—the soundscape has become even more distended owing to the fecundity of the inventors' imagination It has brought into the world piercing beeps, bleeps, tings, plinks, eeks. When the computer appeared, the clatter of the typewriter must have been sorely missed. The hum of the fan in the CPU was an inadequate replacement. Soon a computer purchase included speakers, and the operating system came with a regiment of sound files to better let us know that a folder had been opened, a window reduced, or the trash emptied.

Once more we ought to reflect upon the inescapable conclusion that anything vastly successful or easily and generally accepted sits on the foundation of primordial coding in our collective DNA. In our minds noise conjures energetic, meaningful, companionable activity; it reassures us that we are with and of the world. However, as is so often the case with us imperfect creatures, we do go overboard occasionally. So it is that industrial and post-industrial noise can actually cause harm. Jackhammer operators are supposed to wear ear protectors. Rock musicians and their faithful audiences risk their listening acuity every time the

Noise

amps go up. Executions by shotgun of blaring stereos—occasionally even of their owners—are periodically mentioned in the media.

Humans, no matter in what age or in what culture, have managed to produce plenty of loud noises for ceremonial and/or celebratory affairs. Here as well noise has an intoxicating effect whether on the audience or on the noise-makers. Chanting, clapping hands, beating on hollow wood not only passes the time until the boar is roasted to a turn but reinforces the feeling of tribal belonging. Announcing the birth of a royal heir by shooting off canons not only makes for an effective commercial advertising the ruler's potency but presumably also frightens away the evil spirits. And listening to five thousand[*] voices fervently sing ancient hymns brings goosebumps to the arm and tears to the eye. But we seldom leave well enough alone! If one tenor thrills our innards, concerts with three of them should thrill us threefold.

Our predilection to expect that *more* will automatically also be *better* plays into the whimsy, as it were, of our phenomenal inventiveness. This urge to make a grab for the possible—without asking whether it's necessary—has, more often than not, unintended consequences. In this case one of those consequences happens to be the ever increasing output of ever louder sounds. Today we not only have machines to *make* noises for us; we are able to turn knobs, click levers, or push buttons to *amplify* those noises beyond anything mere

---

[*] Welch voices, unrehearsed, at the Royal Albert Hall, May 3, 1972

nature or people can generate. But even where there is no such button, we live with unintended results. The lawnmower comes to mind. It's a deafening noise that accompanies an otherwise benign activity, that of cutting blades of grass to an even length.

Speaking of a gentle chore: what's with the (leaf) blower? Admittedly, blowing detritus into a heap is faster than raking or sweeping the same amount with muscle power. One suspects, however, that it is not only efficiency that has made this machine so ubiquitous. It might be empowering in not quite obvious ways to use a stinking, roaring, 20kg backpack to blow wilted leaves or cigarette butts into a pile.[*] A bamboo rake's scrape, in contrast, is easily drowned out by a passing car or a barking dog. It fails, therefore, to broad-cast industriousness, virtue, one's very existence to the world.

Listening elsewhere, one also puzzles trying to determine whether it is comforting or alarming to be pierced and thereby awakened, in the dead of night, by the shrill wail of the police car or fire engine siren. Why wake folks within a 20 block radius when the streets tend to offer free sailing at 2 am? Well, these carryings-on proclaim that bad guys and fires are being fought even as we sleep. The blare is comforting. Police and firefighters have advertised to the community that they are on the job. The taxpayer in us can actually hear that some of our money is spent judiciously. We can turn over and drift back to dreamland.

---

[*] Might it not be that, after all that blow-hose lifting, the operator drives to the gym to work on his pecs? Would he not have Arnold-pecs if his arms worked a rake?

Noise

Now that we know that our collective past encourages us to feel good when surrounded by noise, nay, even to groove to its vibrations, it makes perfect sense that cranked-up decibels provide entertainment. More often than not, "louder is better" rules. Take the movies! First spooled while silence prevailed, then while a lonely piano plinked, soon kisses as well as cuffs were accompanied by crashing crescendos on the Wurlitzer organ. Stereophonic surround-sound, cranked up to rock-concert levels, threatens with annihilation not only whatever is standing upright on the screen but also the viewers' ear drums. The entertaining fiddles which delighted generations of dancers in barns and halls have become the amplified electric guitars. Despite amplification, they are often drowned out by their audience's yelling, hooting, hullabalooing.

To change venues as well direction: we did make it to the moon; why can't we build a whisper-quiet lawn mower, jack hammer, motorbike, vacuum cleaner, power saw? Because deep down we don't seem to be wired to really, really want whisper-quiet gadgets. A nearly noiseless lawnmower and a super-quiet vacuum cleaner were invented in Sweden and in Germany respectively during the 1970s. Neither made the slightest dent in the market. The men didn't think that the mowers did a good job, and the Hausfrauen were convinced that most of the dirt had been left behind. Fact cannot argue with perception!

If you can hardly hear the thing, how can you judge its potency? Hmmm ... could this noise thing we have be about sex, pro-creation, creation? Reasonable acquaintance with animal documentary footage leaves no doubt that, by and large, warm-blooded animals carry on fearsomely in the noise-making department when they wish to announce their intent to mate. This may explain why it is primarily the 15 - 28 year old male cohort of our evolutionary line that takes mufflers off cars, tortures motorbikes, engenders permanent loss of hearing in boom-cars. Ear-splitting screams issue forth from females when they are moved to demonstrate their passion for the latest teen-idol. In all genders mile-high amplifiers and electronically enhanced human gutturals produce orgiastic frenzy.

But back to the all-purpose din of daily life! The perception that clamorous noise is an indicator for efficient productivity was reinforced and legitimized during the industrial-mechanical age. Wheels interlocking, gears turning, metal against metal, that sort of thing did turn out the goods. The more things change, the more they stay the same. The association between noise and effect, noise and power seems impervious to technological or cultural changes.

Two and a half electronic decades may have made us dwellers in the global village but they have not ushered in the noise-levels of village life of old. If low-noise performance by our gadgets were our sincere goal, a deep-seated need, or culturally amenable, we'd be able to hear ourselves think now that a lot of them are chip-driven. Truth is that our wiring does not permit us to believe that an operation is in progress if it's not announced or accompanied by a noise. The marketplace's milling consumers respond best to devices which have noise emitters added even where they don't influence the functioning one whit.

Witness the microwave oven. Still in our evolutionary mode of about 10,000 years ago (about 500 generations) and, therefore, being geared for conditions so totally unlike those prevailing now, no consumer groundswell has arisen to force appliance makers to install "noise-off" or "no noise" buttons. The microwave oven has a humming fan and a clicking turntable. Yet we don't trust the thing to be finished when the noise of those mechanical parts stops. We demand at least three consciousness-piercing screeches to tell us that our command to heat whatever for 187 seconds has been executed.[*] We don't even trust ourselves (?) or the microwave (?)—do we know which we don't trust?—to realize that the number buttons work. Each time we press a button, we hear a beeeeeep. Why? It's not telling us that we pressed the wrong or right button! It's only telling us that we did, indeed, press a button!

As another example of us not trusting noiseless electronic servants, observe the new-age denizen who, 12 feet from his car, activates the lock or unlock mechanism. We invent it but we don't trust it. Without hearing that sharp & loud trill, we're convinced that our command hasn't "taken". And let's not obscure the issue by claiming that we hold a [car]

---

[*] For those who have to leave the kitchen while this appliance runs, let's have a timer-button with a sound, but a sound preferably pitched an octave lower than what the thing emits now. Only about eight people in the entire world live in a house big enough to worry that the sound might not carry to where they are.

AHA! ✧ 91

locator! Ask yourself this one question: would this doodad have found the car in the parking garage for Jerry, Elaine, George, Kramer[*]?

The various trills, beeps, grinds, gnashings, whooshings, quacks and burps supplied with every marvel of electronic/digital computer software also hark back to our past. We want to own a slave or two, and we want to know that they have heard our command. That's why we like to hear those squeaks from the ATM when we key in our PIN even though one can plainly see on the bank machine's screen that the thing is responding. That's why we want to hear that "do-re-mi" when we put the key into the car ignition. Only 100 years ago, in the time of our great-grandparents, "yes, Madam" or "very good, Sir!" was the noise expected from a servant. No doubt, the "yes"-quaking slave made our pulse quicken during those formative millennia when our help around the cave or the yurt came from having raided other tribes. That short, unvarying response conveyed that the assignment had been understood and was about to be carried out! Today the same rush hits us upon hearing our mechanical or electronic vassals answer obediently.[†]

---

[*] *Seinfeld* episode 23; Season 3. (For non-*Seinfeldians*: four people are trying to find their car in a high-rise parking garage.)

[†] If the gizmo, however, is not our servant but our master, we're quick to rebel. Disconnecting the buzzer warning that the seatbelt has not been fastened became an ubiquitous weekend project when the safety devices first became mandatory.

Noise

Another dimension of our addiction to noise is just as ancient. To hear a noise that we can reliably associate with a fellow human being tells us that we are not alone. To get separated (for whatever reason) from one's tribe in those far away ages meant almost certain death. A person completely thrown on their own resources could not do everything necessary for survival: hunt regularly and successfully, keep the fire going day & night, guard against carnivorous animals or human enemies *and* get some sleep, survive injury or sickness, secure shelter, make clothes, shape tools, put by provisions. Add that we are intensely social creatures. Banishment from the tribe, ex-communication from the flock of the faithful, sending the snit on the factory floor to Coventry—over the ages the act of "casting out" consigned the "cast-out" to live without the comfort of the human voice and noise. The evidence is better than anecdotal that the casting-out often led to madness or suicide.

We're not at ease with or by ourselves: punishment in prison is the isolation cell; punishment in the home is "time-out"; punishment in the workplace is the silent treatment.[*] So, today those many who are alone the most, or the most alone, are saved from going quietly mad by pushing buttons to create creature comfort through noise. The alienated teenager uses the boom box (a sub-category of which is the

---

[*] Hermits notwithstanding. Human myths in all cultures include stories of solitary persons who, while utterly alone in some inhospitable landscape, resist various temptations, thrive on deprivation, and emerge as sages. Reflection and the getting of wisdom are not associated with the racket of daily life.

Noise

aptly named "ghetto blaster"). No longer in the swim, the senior activates a facsimile of the chattering tribe by turning on the TV upon rising and falls asleep to its reassuring murmur. The weekend-outdoorser vrooms his skidoo in the vast and empty snowscape. It's a form of whistling in the dark … now done *for* us and technologically amplified.

By making rather loud noises we think that, somehow, our unremarkable, anonymous, largely invisible modern selves will be noticed. Think of the youngish persons in our midst. Finally alone in that ultimate badge of adulthood, the car, they fill that miniature cave on wheels with the most tiger-chasing, enemy-scaring, adrenaline-pumping noise, a noise, moreover, in which the bass tones—resembling the trampling and snorting of an enormous as well as outraged beast—make cars in the next lane tremble!

Think of the guy who works by himself on a car project and has the stereo blasting on high alert, yes, alerting the entire neighbourhood to his virtue in maintaining his mode of transportation. Were he living in the kind of tribal 40 to 120 person community of much of our past, everyone would know—or be told about it—that he's working, what he's working on, how good a job he's doing, who is helping him, and that, indeed, it's a good thing that the tribe includes so fine a member. No need to crank up noise to advertise his excellent taste in music, his incredible industry, the incontrovertible fact that he exists. Women advertise their value as well! Doors and windows of their single detached dwelling open, they fill or empty the dishwasher with such elan, lay the table with such finality, vacuum with such

Noise

fervor that neighbours and passers-by are left in no doubt as to the existence of the industrious one within.

Completely tuckered out from all the assertions of power, busyness, existence, we cannot sleep. Besides we're kept awake because too many folk outside the bedroom insist on making known the fact of their existence, revving motorbikes, putting pedal to the metal, saying good-bye for 17 minutes at 2 in the morning on top of their voices, shouting at barking dogs, switching on the siren's wail. Your house lies under a flight-path; your street is the first one on the garbage route; your neighbour warms up his engine (and not just in January) for 13 minutes Monday to Friday at 4:45 am.

Technology comes to the rescue! Go forth then to kill noise with noise: purchase for a very reasonable amount of currency a **Noise Generator**. Its prominent come-on is: *Sleep Better With A White-Noise Generator!* The noises offered to drown out noise are: heartbeat; softsound; rain; great outdoors; ocean waves; brook. Irony of ironies: we evolve alongside nature's noises. Then we make tools that drown out the sounds of nature. In the 3rd millennium we push "the sleep enhancement" button to have nature-noises veil civilization-noises. We're clicking right into our hunter-gatherer brains.

And that same brain will, for quite a few centuries yet, compel nearly every global worldler to crave noise, love noise, make noise. It's noise that assures us that we are in and of this world; it's noise that lets us believe that we can forestall the eternal silence of the grave.

Hair

> **hair** (hâr), n.   1. any of the numerous fine, usually cylindrical filaments growing from the skin of man and animals.
>> The Random House Dictionary of
>> the English Language

As we get more and more urbanized and technologized, we are also getting further and further away from the veldt, the cave, the farm. Hair and fur could disappear tomorrow and we'd not be the worse for it. Assured food supply, comfortable transportation, entertainment in abundance, indoor flush toilets, and chemistry's miracles let most of us live lives which resemble those formerly found only in fairytales or science fiction. Yet the G-force of this forward thrust—fueled by the brain—leaves our innards, our gut feelings, pressed against the tailbone. And attached to that bone, which once upon dawn-of-the-mammal time had a furry appendage growing from it, is our irrational infatuation with hair. We crave a connection to those wooly furry hairy times when lots and lots of those filaments literally surrounded our body. In times when we need neither hairy animals nor hairy noggins for survival, modern civilization spends many billion of dollars on pets and more billions yet on what we still consider our crowning glory.

That a rising standard of living brings a concomitant rise in the pet population can be observed today in China, India, Japan as well as right under our running shoes! At the same time, living better also supports a vast industry that disgorges torrents of better products to pet our own hair with. This confluence of indulgences points compellingly to our common heritage, far away though it may seem. Because it was the domestication of the wolf which came before the domestication of bad hair, pet thought-yarn will be spun out first. Why is it, for instance, that we feel calm, comfort, a belly-kind of well-being when we run our fingers through the fur of a dog or cat? Reflections on our inclination to run fingers through human hair shall come second as befits our species who appeared long, long after four-footed mammalians had the run of the globe.

The connection between the supermarket meat counter and Rex, the shepherd dog, seems tenuous. However, it is not. Before the wolf was tamed to become a dog[*] and thousands of generations before those wolf-descendants were bred to produce (reliably) litters of dogs that were able assistants in the herding of sheep and goats, a wolf was, first and foremost, food, glorious food! Any furry creature was food and life and survival. The meat was essential. But the rest was all made use of as well: blood, bones, sinew, innards, teeth, brain, horns, tusks, the skin. These utilitarian items were a bonus that came with the meat. The skin, the animal's fur coat, however, must have carried in addition a whiff of extra comfort, even luxury.

When the hunters returned with even only a rabbit, it would be skinned and the fur used for some artifact to wrap around feet. That by-product of the food item made it less painful to

---

[*] The taming—genetic modification, actually—of wolves happened about 12,000 years ago.

Hair

walk over spiny ground cover, scree, or snow. If not for footwear, the women would prize the rabbit fur for making carrying-bags or capes for babies. And what a warm glow must have arisen in our ur-moms when they contemplated the hairy pelt of aurochs, wooly mammoth, bear, deer, antelope, mountain goat, or wolf! Even before any of these animals had been skinned, one could imagine the hide as clothing, footwear, mattress, blanket, tent covering, pouches, hats. Before the advent of textiles, fur and bark-strips were the fabric of all wearage. Since woven cedarbark T-shirts are not a commercial item but fur-wear is, one may assume that we're inclined in our very nature to prefer pelt to wood fibre.

In the northern climates to which some of our ancestors migrated, in frozen Siberia with its almost endless winters, during the last ice age (which saw the appearance of homo sapiens sapiens), we had plenty of reason and plenty of time to get a favourable response to fur built into us. Instinctively most of us welcome sunshine and, toward its warmth, stretch our arms in a feeling of sudden well-being. Instinctively most of us welcome a four-legged fur-wrapped life form and, toward its cozy pelt, stretch our fingers.

Fur and food loomed equally large as life-sustaining, life-enhancing. Both came in one package. Animals existed to be killed, skinned, eaten, their bones and pelts made use of. However, this is being written on an electronic word processor and not with a goose-quill because our species loves to imagine, invent, and improve. We are not good at leaving well enough alone. Not leaving well enough alone meant that the use of animals soon bifurcated. One branch remained as the food supply, the other became the domesticated resource.

Our evolutionary ancestors changed their hitherto unvarying relationship to animals. They actually re-designed life by taming their food supply. Tamed, the food, under those ever so useful pelts, was kept close by and needed no longer hunting down with spear or arrow. The well-bred wolf and some amenable birds were kept inside dwellings. Later, goats, cows, horses were added to the menagerie which, until very recently, still shared the roof with their owners. One could, and did, sleep next to the furry beast to be warmed by its soft hairy covering.

Many of the creatures could be trained as companion, hunting "tool", guard, protector, and serve as lightning rod for temper tantrums. The winged assets gave eggs, readily available meat, feathers for adornment. Some birds even hunted with and for their master. Genetically modified, consumer-designed pets were not long in coming. From day one of domestication we've bred dogs, cats, birds to get the better product. Dogs for hunting, pointing, shepherding; cats for mousing, petting, looks; birds for egg-laying, homeing, hunting. As far back as then we've been intrigued by, and probably were willing to pay for, different "designs".

Whatever the looks of the creature, from that first bonding between human and animal onward, we've often had a closer relationship with a dog or cat than with other human beings. One reason for feeling so close to our non-verbalizing pet may be that talking came last for us in our evolution, and that talking is so brain-based. Having an animal around and communicating in the most basic of ways with this other being comes from somewhere deep in us, somewhere were we don't get to go much in the talk-drenched world we've made. Today, in an environment bereft of truly immediate "do this or starve" experiences, having a dog or feline links us subconsciously and atavistically to a less complex past, the past for which we're still tuned.

Tuned, as we still are, to feel warm and secure when close to a pelt, we understand how otherwise sane and compassionate persons lose all perspective and take a dog into homes that are too small, lives that are too busy, lives that no longer demand or need working dogs or mousing cats. The dog was domesticated to be a helpmate. Trained to guard sheep, pigs, or goats, sniff out game, retrieve kill, chase foxes, exterminate vermin, lie in the meadow but bound toward us when we whistle, pull carts, sleep in the barnyard, kill gophers, they led a life outside, outside, outside! But, then, that is, until around the middle of the 19th century, most of us lived a great deal more outside as well.

Lately we've moved from the great outdoors into the small indoors to earn our daily bread. A consequence—one expected from a large-brained, logic-capable, urbanized humanid—is that our cherished and petted workmate has become *the pet*. It's a pet's job to do nothing except play, entertain, and visibly enjoy the owner's affectionate attention. For the past few decades it has been the human that works to feed the dog. Almost all pet chow is advertised

Hair

as nourishing not only for the body of the darling but also for its fur. And so the human has brought forth, and has happily turned into a huge success, a billion dollar pet food industry which, among other assurances, promises us the sight of a healthy, lustrous, thick coat of hair upon the body of our beloved quadruped.

Our love affair with lots of hair—curly, straight, long, short, thick, fine—is not confined to pets. We love to see lots of hair on ourselves, to wrap ourselves right into it. As far back in time as we know, certain furs were status symbols. In Africa the skin of a leopard was draped artfully over the upper body of a chieftain; in Europe rank, position, status could be deduced from the number of black spots—which only the weasel's tail end could supply—in the ermine trim on the robes of officials such as kings, peers of the realm, or judges. In cold climates fur coats, fur hats, fur collars, fur muffs, fur-lined clothing and footwear are, of course, also practical because incredibly warm. Nevertheless, the status thing comes with the merchandise. The right kind of fur advertises the approximate wealth of the wearer.

While the dead-pelt business has declined, the live-pelt industry thrives. If Americans alone spend $5 billion a year just on dog food and $7 billion on having their sweetums doctored, the world-wide amount spent must rival that of the gross national product of a decent-sized country. Not counted in those billion figures are such fascinating items as pet cemeteries, pet camps, pet grooming parlors, pet clothes, pet toys, pet walkers, pet sitters, pet daycare, pet spas, pet contests, pet breeders, flea collars, ID tags, electric fence systems, dog and cat houses, dog and cat shampoo, the SPCA behemoth. Actually, little escapes the pet owner as doable for her/his beloved. If one mentions pet psychiatrists, pet crystal feeding dishes, and pet birthday party arrangers, the need of the naked ape for a furry animal companion announces itself in a blinding flash. Nothing is as appealing, satisfying, downright happy-making than those soft, warm, smelly patches of fur that have round eyes to look at you, four legs to run toward you, and a wet nose to nuzzle against you. And no voice box to talk back at you! The Pet Loss Bereavement Counselor is trained to understand all that.

The more our technology makes us well-off, the more we can indulge our primal impulses. Spending billions on the care and feeding of fur-bearing critters is trumped many times over by the billions spent on the care and, yes, feeding of what's left of our fur. Our locks, curly or straight, wavy or wiry, are the remnants of our thick body hair, our fur. And since we are attracted to all features that promise good genes and/or maximum survival potential for our own DNA, the full head of hair, no doubt, tweaks our coding in ways that are not obvious today.

In ages when we did not yet know how to modify our environment to be warm in winter or cool in the summer, hair conferred protection from freezing to death or having one's skin roasted. The taming of fire, using caves as shelter, building primitive huts and keeping a source of heat going took almost 300,000 years. Over that time body hair became less and less necessary to keep the DNA container alive long enough to produce a version of itself. Speaking of

those replicas: every baby replica found the nourishing
nipple beneath some hair, be it the fur or hair of the mom
unit or her chest-covering furry garb. That primal memory
alone should suffice to make us want to touch, stroke, nuzzle
hair.

It seems that people in all cultures treasure a full head of hair
without actually sitting down to think about the reasons.[*]
Hair is used as one's "treasure", something that we value
because it identifies us. It signals to others who we are and
that we are. And the "that we are" is connected to our
identity. Our hair really does "represent" our person. And
every person wants/needs to leave her/his DNA. Which is
why what hair looks like to the world sends signals about
mating. One does not have to look far to find this (subconscious) connection at work.

So, for instance, right into the 20th century some cultures
scalped their enemies or shrunk their cut-off heads.
Conveniently the hair provided a built-in thong with which
to fasten the memento upon the victor's belt. A more
valuable trophy than a mere clavicle-bone or shrumpled ear,
the hairy scalp represented the vanquished person. That
person, an enemy, obviously could no longer produce
offspring.

The warp of many of our culture's myths is our reproductive
urge while the weave is spun of images of powerful hair.

---

[*] Even if the hair is purposely shorn, cut back to stubbles, or pinned
back, that very act is making a statement about what grows at the top of
one's person.

Hair

There's Samson, only strong until shorn of his hair; Maria Magdalene, repenting her sexual past, drying Jesus' feet with her hair; Lady Godiva, shielding her chastity with the mantle of her own hair; Rapunzel whose hair becomes the ladder her lover prince climbs to enter her turret; Salome, who swirled her seven veils seductively to get her vengeance-wish: John The Baptist's bleeding head, under a full shock of hair, on a platter.

Hair is so problematical! For one thing—actually the main thing, as we've seen already—hair sends subliminal sexual messages. As if that were necessary! We all know and say out loud that lots of healthy hair is sooo sexy. Advertising manages to take full advantage of our fascination with, attraction to, longing for a magnificent head of hair. Advertising builds on what we do or respond to already. A woman's face becomes more lovely when surrounded by fur; a man looks, well, manly in a fur toque. The sex, drugs, rock'n-roll 1960s and '70s were remarkable for the sheer quantity of long hair displayed by the coming-of-age generation. Their hirsute appearance not only advertised defiance of convention but also signaled their rebellion against the sexual mores on the parental side. That particular generation cut its collective hair as it entered and succeeded in the business world, some even shaving off all head hair. The deliberately bald ones, oh perversity!, are often thought of as incredibly sexy, presumably because they literally shine with self-confidence. Yet to have one's hair shorn forcibly by an enemy is a form of degradation and punishment.

Hair

Hair is so problematical! How many women moan that those whom they have bewitched and by whom they are charmed make impossible demands on their hair! Men, they say, never want hair short. Men babble about long hair through which they can run their fingers, hair that streams in the wind, hair that falls in soft waves about their woman's face and shoulders and neck and ears. Women's preference for the guy with a healthy shock of hair is not in dispute. They may, however, when confronted with thinning hair on the male's pate but a thick wallet in his pocket, change their minds. (Maybe he employs a chauffeur with a great head of hair?)

Women's hair is problematical because the long and lots of it seems atavistically linked to sexuality. It's what beneath those flowing strands that must somehow be kept hidden or underneath a cover! In one culture, the chador hides the hair and its promise. Without that head of hair, a singularly defining feature, veiled women look all alike. It's only the owner who gets to unveil, to unwrap, his very own possession. In another culture, a veil covers the bride's face until the groom, at that point her lawfully wedded husband, lifts it to kiss her on the mouth. Nuns, bound by a vow of chastity, used to get their hair cut off and what was left of it covered by the religious order's black veil.

Hollywood provides another, albeit more complex, unveiling of the sexual creature in "ceremonies" fitted to the temper of the times. Melanie Griffith in *Working Girl* has, as secretary, what she herself calls "Mall hair". When she decides to climb the ladder of success, her first move is to

Hair

acquire "serious hair" by cutting off the long curly stuff. In case we miss the tribal visual way of classification here: the secretaries she leaves behind have long hair; the senior executives she joins have short hair.

In scores of other movies, the ladder of success—which in these flicks means getting out of the office and into a stay-at-home marriage with the head-honcho of the whole shebang—is climbed by changing the short hair to long. Since picture frames on celluloid started unrolling, the scenario unfolds something like this. The mousy female is an underling of some sort in an entrepreneurial organization. She usually wears skirts too long, glasses too thick, shoes too clunky. Her hair is tied in a bun or otherwise mangled. Of course she has all the qualities prime DNA carriers for the next generation should exhibit: she's ultra-efficient, warm-hearted, intelligent; orderly; industrious. Owing to the finessing of the plot, the male protagonist—always higher on the prestige scale than our mouse—asks her to accompany him in a social setting. Fade out!

Blend in! Mouse appears in a dress with a short hemline or in a long gown with décolletage; the glasses are gone; the feet shod in Cinderella slippers ... with high heels. That thou shalt not judge a book by its cover (the underlying moral of the story among other morals!) becomes blazingly clear when the male lead and everyone in the audience is bedazzled by the veritable cascade of luxuriant hair that had been hidden in that little bun! **The End** is satisfying because we have seen the triumph of passion, signified by the hair set free, and the ancient ritual in which girl gets rich

Hair

boy. She let him free her prize possession from those restraining pins.

Movies, which are not myth-making but myth-embellishing, have been ably augmented by television. A perfectly droll example of how we just can't shake our coding is the late 1990s blossoming of hair-related signals. Its manifestation started in a serious way when Nell, aka "Sub-Zero" on *Ally McBeal* appeared. She's fabulously clever, editor of a Harvard law journal, gorgeously tall, Boticelli-faced and, of course, blond, a hair colour that pushes another button. She has her tresses pinned in a severe bun. As do all the female lawyers in the firm, Nell feels entitled to want it all. She goes into mating mode and hits on The Biscuit (if you have to ask, don't; just read along as if "his" name were Bob or something). He needs major signals of her intentions. What better flag to wave, as it were, than to loosen her hair and swish it seductively in front of him, right in his office.

During that televised celebrity orgy, the Hollywood Oscars of the same season, over 100 million persons all over the world got to see quite a few actors of the female persuasion in flowing gowns and extravagant jewels but with their hair gathered in severe buns. Every pulled-back strand of hair got immediately tied to our movie memories of dowdy librarians metamorphosing into ball-gowned, flowing-hair crowned beauties. The visual clue synergy between actors and worldwide audience came at a time when technology—brain-over-brawn jobs, the pill, mechanical & chemical household help—had freed women from their children,

Hair

kitchen, church fetters. That massive amounts of rivuletting hair live under that tidy bun taps into some great fantasies.

- women want to, and can, have it all: the career as well as the mate & babies
- men don't mind the career if the long hair is hidden rather than bobbed
- it's a guess but one that's probably spot-on: over 90% of all men have hair fetishes and hate to have "their" woman cut her hair
- both, men and women, prove that they are a business/law/administrative genius, severe and totally with the digital age, by having their hair as tightly controlled as their emotions
- both, men and women, are programmed to adore hair since it is tied to the beginning of mammalian life, to the beginning of our species' life, to the beginning of our individual lives, to warmth, to comfort, to sex, and (subliminally) to food under fur
- one yank on a pin causes an undulating mass of golden or raven-black tendrils to cascades about face and over shoulders thereby utterly transforming the beloved
- men: unhook a fastener and Ms Restrained will turn into Ms Passion
- women: unhook the fastener and see the real me !!!

It's bracing to realize that the female TV personality—talk-show host, interview queen, cook, household specialist, anchor, reporter—has hair that's cut to about ear-lobe level. This is a fine compromise between womanly hair-allure and the gender-neutral professional look. Looks count! Looks

Hair

tell us primitives at a glance what to expect from the "gestalt". As well we clue into how to adapt our behaviour so we will get along with that person (assuming that is our goal). The notion that "one cannot tell a book by its cover" is a notion born of the print culture. Were this proverbial "wisdom" true to our wiring, every volume on bookstore shelves would look like its neighbour! Our quick responses are still almost exclusively to iconic visual stimuli. Consequently, the bodacious, babebocious hair-head cavorts on *Baywatch* but does not comment on the evening news.

And so it happens that advertising, ever trying to click into our deepest fantasies and longings, plays on our fur/hair worship to the hilt. Wherefore the allure of thick-maned goddesses, mostly fair-haired, their veritable manes swirling in cleverly lit commercials. These partially voiced but predominantly visual mini-narratives tell of magic potions which will free us, everyone, from our worst nightmare: the bad hair day! It cannot be a coincidence that when we feel strung out in these high-tech times, we express our dis-ease with a phrase instinctively understood by us ex-fur-covered creatures: "bad hair day!".

Fantasies deal with possibilities and not with probabilities. Although what transpires in a commercial will never be our real-life experience, the scenarios are possible and so we respond to the goings-on. The best advertising arises from the same place where the ad-designer hopes it will make its impact in the consumer. However, that place can only be stumbled upon, witness the relatively few ads that transcend the product while making the pitch. One such ad blends hair

Hair

(fur) with speed (horse), iron maiden (armour), and the promise of sex (lots of flowing hair). This is it: the babe, dressed from head to toe in black leather, alights from her steed, the Harley, removes her severe motorbike helmet and—whoosh!—swings her golden tresses with a provocative beckoning of the head.

That motorcycle ride and dismount is a long way from shampooing one's hair. It's not about hair anyway; it's about mating. And that is why a goodly portion of hair dollars are being spent in the male domain as well. General obsessing about hair is gender-neutral. George Costanza's receding hairline provided many an episode, wailings, crises. *Seinfeld*, after all, addressed itself to the "nothing" concerns of the baby boom generation, the very generation that took hair, lots of it and long, as a badge of identification with, yes, "letting one's hair down". George gave expression to the angst his demographic cohort began to feel at the stage in one's life cycle when mortality stares one in the face as one holds that first dead, white, fallen hair in hand. From where we know not arises the dread that the falling of hair portends the decline of virility.

Into this dismay slinks another advertising effort. Imprinted upon the retina of every magazine- or newspaper-reading person on this earth is the "Before" and "After" photo of the hair-challenged male head. First that pathetic shot of a shiny scalp with 127 hairs draped in 9 rows across it so as to fool the beholder into thinking there's coverage. Then the "After" picture with hair so luscious, so curly, so extensive

Hair

that one's fingers—were they not holding the paper—might well reach out to rummage through that thicket of fur!

Something about that "thicket" though. We're intolerant of smallish amounts of hair. Totally bald is o.k.; as noted before, guys with shiny domes often look awesomely sexy. What is culturally not ok is a sprinkling of hair, so to speak. One year short of the millennium, the "Julia Roberts' underarm-hair incident" occurred. While Julia is iconized with a nice shock of hair on her head, we will not allow the merest tuft elsewhere on her body. The furore erupted over a major event appearance for which she was dressed "beautifully" in a long sheath-type affair with high neckline but without sleeves. She raised one arm to wave at her adoring fans. And, gasp!!!, she had fur under her arm! Tons of folk beheld a furry armpit. All hell broke loose. Castigating comments issued forth from screen and print; one could have thought her Hester Prynne revealing the "A" to the masses. This reaction, no doubt, drew forth even more dollar billions spent on that piece in the cosmetic pie chart that is devoted to the removal of hair, smallish amounts of hair on upper lip, on chin, on legs, on arms, below the belly button. Well, yes, shaving off head or body hair with whatever precursors to the safety razor was also practiced by those stone-age tribes which survived into the 20th century.

Looking forward to the 31st century or even the 56th, as science fiction is wont to do, we see women and men mostly bald or with their heads permanently covered. If they are of our species, they are bald. If they are of a superior, but alien, species, they are bald. If they join the human race, they

AHA! ✧ 112

Hair

acquire hair while keeping other home-planet characteristics. If they are giant brains pulsating with super-human intelligence, they are bald. ET is hairless and so is that creature in the Roswell, New Mexico footage. The aforementioned weavings of our imagination use the thread of our evolution from furry to naked ape. The more evolved, the less hair. The less evolved, the more hair. It's unlikely that at sci-fi conventions writers and illustrators conspire to assign body hair or hairy appendages only to those species found in "underdeveloped" galaxies far, far away!

The glimpse upon future human daily life presented by sci-fi is definitely deficient in the shaggy, furry, four-legged sector. Quickly now, who can recall a book, an illustration, a movie or a TV series in which either we or the aliens had real pets for the length of the tale? The *Star Trek* "Tribbles" episode illustrates perfectly the point that those who dream of human advancement (and those who go along for the ride) imagine a future without hair or fur. In that episode, the irrational appeal of those adorable little fur-balls leads the crew to indulge the pets to the point where their exponential propagation threatens the very survival of *The Enterprise*. The death of beastly hair in science fiction is but another bead in the strand of our ambivalence about hair. Somewhere in our collective unconscious, reinforced through countless illustrations, lives evil in the shape of the devil, he of the horns, the tail, and the hair all over. Angels, of course, even the male archangels, have wavy light-coloured hair. Elsewhere their bodies are as hairless as a piece of marble.

Hair

The naked ape spends billions on shavers, creams, electrolysis, wax, depilatory concoctions for anything beneath the eyebrows. For what's above them, billions of dollars are exchanged for tonsorial services, potions, shampoos, rinses, dyes, fluids that will curl, fluids that will de-curl, growth tinctures, thickening lotions, whiteners, brighteners, highlighteners. This amusing inconsistency mirrors the conflict between good and bad ... no less. By getting rid of body hair we believe we can rid ourselves of our furry ape relationship, of our primordial impulses.

Not that we aren't powerfully attracted to hair; that much we know when we look at our very own 21st century tribbles everywhere. In the world that the naked ape has invented, little speaks to our still intact hunter-gatherer instincts. Let's indulge our fixation upon hair & fur in all manifestations that make our world turn. Science-fiction and human suspicion of hairy humans notwithstanding, all mammals have hair. Even the whale has a few bristles. And hair is about mating, mating is about speciation, speciation is about "infinite diversity in infinite combinations", and one combination produced us. Enjoy your pet; theirs and our filaments are of the same composition.

Magic

> **magic** (maj′ik), n.   1. the art of producing a
> desired effect or result through the use of
> various techniques, as incantation, that
> presumably assure human control of
> supernatural agencies or the forces of nature.
>
> The Random House Dictionary of the
> English Language

Our ubiquitous, subconscious belief in magic is the link
between the billion dollar consumption of fast food and
many other modern miracles besides. The connection lies in
the fibres which make up a long and resilient thread woven
since time immemorial. That thread has never been severed
and still ties us to

1.   faith that magic can/may resolve whatever difficulty,
2.   confidence that the human brain can/may pull the
     magic rabbit out of the hat
3.   evolutionary benefits for those who kept going
     because they did not doubt 1. and 2.

Where there is hope, there is life. Most of this chapter is
about today's magic, as in "the art of producing a desired
effect or result through the use of various *technology*". What
will be examined first is the miraculosity of fast food; what
other products human ingenuity has conjured will be after-
meal entertainment, as it were. Food comes first because it's
easier to find magical that soft, sweet, semi-frozen cream
heaps itself from a machine-spout into a baked, cone-shaped
waffle than it is to marvel at, say, that electricity needs a (+)
and a (−) to get a kettle boiling.

Magic

Fast food is proof of magic in our age. In many parts of the world, the spectre of going 72 minutes without a snack has been banished. A meal can be ordered in less than 55 seconds, grabbed to go within 3 minutes, paid for in 1, and eaten in 4. To sink teeth, on the spur of the moment, into a white bun with already minced and cooked meat inside has been 42,578 years in coming but was never—one can be sure—far from humans' imagining and wishing-it-were. Until recently the appearance of a tray with meat, potatoes, bread, salt, pepper, condiment, and foamy, flavoured, sweet milk, at the cost of a fraction of the average hourly wage, would have required the same kind of belief that can accommodate the existence of hovering sprites interested in our fate.

Spoilsports decry the agreeable sorcery of the fast food phenomenon and snort that what's conjured is not nourishing food. Yet, compared to the pickings or offerings of by-gone ages right up to the early 20th century, a wrap, a submarine, a pizza, a BLT, a hamburger with that one lettuce leaf would have provided more balanced nutrition than do potatoes morning, noon, and night or hot porridge, fried porridge, cold porridge with that wee bit of honey—*maybe* honey, *maybe* milk. During those times the terms "quality control", "nutritional analysis", "list of ingredients" would have encountered an uncomprehending stare. Never mind that what many today consider down-market food, would have, in other times, ranked as a fine meal for chief or aristocrat.

In 1567 Pieter Breughel painted *The Land of Cockaigne*, named after that fairytale place where the already roasted pigeons fly into the visitor's open mouth. He fancifully presents the daydreams which kept heart and mind of pre-industrial personkind from despairing over the daily chore of having to procure and make palatable a meal. Here's the folk fantasy as presented by Breughel: three totally pigged-out guys lie under a tree. A food-laden table grows right around the tree trunk. The chow is hearty and ready to eat. (The operative word here is "ready".) There's the medieval version of food-on-the-run: a roasted pig with a carving knife sticking in its crispy skin, a bow-legged boiled egg ready to be spooned out, and a sausage-link fence just asking to be dismantled.

This fancy was possible but, at that moment, required magic to materialize. Life was harsh. No supermarket opened its doors reliably every day. No 24/7 convenience store was within walking distance. Gruel and coarse bread ruled. Only in folklore did dishes, sufficient for a three-course meal, appear ready for the eating. The conjurer did not have to plow, sow, rake, hoe, harvest, prepare, cook, and generally perform those far too many steps between what comes of the earth and passes our lips.

During those centuries preceding our own, humans scarcely ever sat down without giving thanks to some deity for what they were about to eat. Neither did they lack ceremonies, throughout the seasons, devised to propitiate whatever forces to let no harm come to the animal herd or grain harvest. Daily meals on a regular, predictable basis, were recognized as a blessing and not taken for granted. It's unsettling to read that unearthed skeletons from a range of centuries—

including the nineteenth—show bones with the tell-tale signs of not just one but sometimes several periods of starvation.

If the availability of food were made into *The Greatest Story Ever Told*, the first 94 minutes would be depressing. There'd be a lot of hunger, minimal food choice or no choice at all, stunted growth because essentials were missing, outright starvation, even cannibalism. The last 13 minutes would not provide a real high either since at that point the footage segues into a grotesque ending. Panning to a stretch of urban space dotted with its outlets of Macdonalds, Pizza-Huts, KFCs we are forced to look at the eye-popping number of obese folk waddling about. A steady stream of humans could be seen gorging themselves on deep-fried potatoes, fried chicken, deep-fried onion rings, fizzy flavoured coloured sugar water, pizza, doughnuts, ice cream, muffins, chips of all kinds, tacos, meat in buns, fish in buns, cheese in buns. Rational thought availeth not against age-old survival instincts. Given a choice between a small sized snack or pop and a supergiganticlargeone, the way biggest number of customers pay for the ginormous portion. Our instincts seems to whisper even now: "lean times just around the corner!"

The magic of having food, and more than enough of it, leap into our laps comes about because we enthusiastically leapt ourselves into the lap of an industry generating billions and billions of dollars and millions of pay-cheques (from which a portion hops back for fries & a shake). The take-out, deliver, drive-in, self-serve, order & grab vittles-business is still growing and will go on growing. Success and swarming of

Magic

bank notes comes to those who intuit what marketing niche sits in the immediate neighbourhood to some ancient genetic coding. The marketing gods have something most basic to work with: the organism's drive to sustain itself. Alimentary! In a race for first place in the hierarchy of life's essentials—food, comfort, money, love, learning, self-actualization—food wins by mile.

That the global marketplace is thronged with folk, hands outstretched, bearing coin in exchange for ready-to-eats happens to hit memory codes embedded in our species. The fantasy is universal that one soweth not, harvesteth not, cooketh not, yet eateth! Whether a band of hunter-gatherers faced another evening having chased but not bagged, foraged but not found or settlers braved another year of a drought, hunger pangs, endured often, were fertile ground for the seed of wishful thinking. It yielded a rather rich harvest of imaginings about instant stomach gratification. The Bible, that fine book that tells all about the agricultural stage, gives us the proverbial "land of milk and honey" and "manna falling from heaven".[*]

The magic of a meal ready in mere minutes casts its spell over cultures that go back a long while. Humans everywhere who can afford the fixings indulge their taste buds with succulent, savory, substantial results of the local cuisine. Nevertheless they also are seduced by the ease with which *"ready-made"* makes mincemeat of *"from scratch"*. Those born before the world-wide triumph of the golden arches will

---

[*] The story of the seven lean and the seven fat years can be found here as well.

Magic

remember that general wisdom that the French would never deign to let deep-fried potato-mash replace their pommes frites. O yeah? Macdonalds hasn't exactly gone broke in France! And a European fast-pizza chain is doing fine in Italy!

Much is to be gained by the entrepreneurs if the money-for-food exchange resembles the waving of a wand. It has to be quicker and less expensive than what one could achieve at home (always factoring in the bother). It does not have to be better-tasting. We wave our wand, as it were, by proffering smallish coin to summon that patty of meat between slices of cheese, all in a bun. But a price has to be paid always. Even here we are much favoured over our ancestors.

The pre-historical price to be paid was leaving a part of the kill, usually a part much desired by the human, for the spirits. Humans or animals were sacrificed (as the price that had to be paid) to ensure a regular food supply from the suitably appeased deity. For Thanksgiving, to this day, some of the bounty of the land is arrayed beautifully before the altars in many churches in many countries to give something in return. A price of a different sort is exacted in the stories about sugar-cake land. Our ancestors who concocted the vision of pancakes growing on roof tops and waffles reclining upon the ground knew that. To reach the land of perpetual salivation in these tales, the travelers have to eat themselves through a mountain of porridge or other gruesome daily fare of real life. One prefers to tender coin.

Magic

Coin is tendered somewhere every second of every day in the empire of food. That coin is tendered because humans have dreams. They invent technology to fulfill and pay for those dreams. And those dreams are built on coding that precedes homo erectus, the apes, the reptile, even whatever swam first. Find food fast; feed fast while the food is there; Fast Food. Although we obviously have the wits to fulfill sundry food dreams, we do not care to employ those smarts nearly as enthusiastically to other imaginings because it's the coding that determines where the resources for inventions go.

The evidence suggests that we are not, for example, coded to dream of fulfilling cerebral quests the same way we are coded to pursue an easier way to stuff ourselves. One is hard pressed to find commercial outlets which, at a minimal cost, let us gorge on having fun doing calculus, listening to études by Chopin, or reading every word of Edward Gibbon's *Decline and Fall of the Roman Empire*. The success of www.amazon.com et al. is based more on our infatuation with that newest tool, the clicky-mouse, in that greener pasture, the Internet, than on a rising love of reading deep books. Marketing directed to the pleasures of thinking is at most a dozen pixels in that rather large bit-map of our gratification snapshot.

"Pixels" is a concept as good as any to trigger moving from the magic we understand—harvest, cook, eat—to the magic we don't. Our creature comforts are based on inventions, processes, material configurations which we do not comprehend nor could re-constitute if the magic failed.

Magic

Aggregates of humans the world over cannot "fix"—assuming their local power grid were destroyed—"electricity". How, confronted with a risen Lazarus from 1772, would I, or you, dear reader, explain to him the workings of "how to boil water"? Plug some metal prongs into holes in the wall. The prongs are connected to a two-foot cord. The cord hangs on what looks like a pitcher full of water. The thing starts to make noises. At this point the 1772 Lazarus may well yell "yikes!" and try to flee. The pitcher emits a shrieking whistle while steam sssshhhhhshs from the pouring spout! Lazarus freaks; you reassure him; pull out the cord; the pitcher simmers down. Lazarus doesn't even want to look! What if that creature that made the water boil comes jumping out of those holes in the wall?

Being cast upon a Robinsonian island we would not know how to replicate a match even though match-magic is a howling success. Everyone has at least one box of matches in their dwelling and knows how to use one. Bereft of this low-tech wonder, how would we start a fire? It's one thing to know that if rapidly rubbed together, two sticks may give off sparks; it's quite another to create a fine splice of wood, concoct some chemical goop with which to tip it, dry it, and sometime later have a flame jump up when scratched against the back of one's jeans. (It gives one pause to realize that neither jeans nor any kind of comfortable trousers could readily be procured on such an island.)

A belief in magic solutions to save us toil and trouble *if only* we say the magic word or make the gesture is another sub-routine somewhere in our cerebrum. This belief brought about the most astonishing proof of the existence of goblins, elves, masters of X. To call them forth to perform their specialty for modern persons, we rather (unceremoniously) perform all manner of rituals. Sacred incantations and "Open Sesame" is no longer our MO[*]; instead we push buttons, kick metal, drop coins, touch flat surfaces, move knobs, flick switches, turn taps, press levers, swipe plastic, turn keys, strike wooden sticks.

And lo!, our pre-historic conviction that magic availeth will soon get another dollop of affirmation. "Open Sesame" will bring the desired result via electronic voice recognition. By 2005 we will, no doubt, utter "bbq on" … whereupon the thing shows its neat rows of tamed flames without us having to go through that toil-some ritual of lighting matches, clicking a starter, or turning a knob! And to think that once upon a time, around 1965, one had to wait (what a concept!) for about 40 minutes to get the charcoal to glow sufficiently to cook one's steak to resemble the roasted kill of circa 150,000 years ago!

Having successfully importuned the gods and the spirit world to bestow upon us a world of ease and plenty, we show little gratitude. Because we do more grumbling than we do appreciating, below a very sketchy reminder that we have, indeed, lost our sense of wonder because magic can be—day-in, day-out—reliably summoned.

---

[*] *modus operandi* (for those who are not quite with today's alphabet soup, also a fast food!)

MAGIC	RABBIT	BEFORE MAGIC
click a remote	controls tv; vcr, stereo; locks, opens car; opens garage door	get up, turn knob, sit back down, stick with one channel. Turn key. Stop car, brake on, get out, walk, turn key, lift garage door, get back into car, brake off, drive
click mouse	get world wide web: send, receive, forward, cc, open mail; listen to music; get the news; get pornography; get a recipe; send an animated card; wade into sports trivia; buy, buy, buy; auction; check out prices; book a vacation; read a newspaper; chat live; post to alt.x; download music, software, games; do research; have your astrological chart done; see the world and all that it contains	leave home, travel take pen, paper; write letter; address envelope; buy & glue on stamp; take to PO or mail box / copy by hand, copy by machine, address envelope(s), frank, lick, close, carry to PO or box read a newspaper: make decision as to buy on whim or subscribe; pick up; sit down; take in hands (which hands will gradually blacken); go to favourite section; let eye fly over every page, skim headlines, skim bold print, zap over visuals, pause to read more or look longer here or there, come across something totally new & unexpected, do crossword, look at horoscope, finish with comics; fold paper; take paper to recycle bin etc. ... elaboration of all the steps necessary to do what the magic mouse-click now brings would take several pages
drop coin into slot	get snacks, hot/cold drinks, stockings, condoms, holy water, subway ticket, juke box music, arcade games, alcohol breath test, any kind of amusement, gumballs, coin change; T-shirt, park; phone; use public washroom; do	hunt; gather; make fire; skin animals; cure, sew hides; gather wool; spin; weave; sew; wash in stream; dry on grass or on line; buy, stable, feed, groom, shoe, saddle horse (no subway); build, string, tune, learn to play instrument + get along with other players to get more than a lonely tune; kill sheep, skin, cure skin, make parchment, take goose quill, sharpen, make ink, dip quill,

	laundry, lose money, win jackpot; copy; weigh yourself; take a photo of yourself; massage your feet … "please deposit 25¢ coin to continue"	copy manuscript; be rich, hire artist, sit still for hours, have him paint you … no end in sight for cumbersome toil
flick switch	shave; beat egg; brew coffee; get bright lights; get warmth; get cooking; vacuum; scumbust; saw; drill; turn screw; drive lathe; grind coffee; cool air, warm air, blow air; swirlpool, whirlpool, clean pool; raise gate, lower gate; mow lawn … save elbow grease	rub sticks together or strike flint-stone; set on fire pitch, oil, tallow, wax, kerosene, gas, wood, rushes, fibre, candle wicks. Constantly maintain wick equivalent. Cut down or gather wood, have kindling, store, dry, bring into house, layer in fireplace or stove, obtain spark, set on fire, cross fingers, use bellows, maintain fire. Expenditure of much toil over long periods of time. [Flick toggle switch in brain to ON to continue with column on your own]
insert plastic; swipe plastic; send number on plastic into cyber-space	pay bills; get cash; transact money matters; bid on e-Bay; buy stuff in the global market place; lock & unlock; phone; get gas; buy movie ticket; park; buy on credit; debit or credit account; use as security pledge; bankrupt yourself;	barter; pretty shells; gold pieces; metal coins; verbal agreement & handshake; precious gem stones; heavy large keys for strong box. Most uses for plastic card not invented until 20th century. "Money in the bank" not relevant since until around 1930 most people never even saw the inside of a bank. The pay packet with cash in it did not fade into memory until the 1980s.

MAGIC	RABBIT	BEFORE MAGIC
push or touch button	1. orchestra plays 2. Aunt Ethel says "hello", you say "hi" to her 3. rise to 11th floor 4. wash dishes 5. wash laundry 6. flush toilet 7. heat oven to correct temperature	1. cave days: does not exist; 17th cent: be rich enough to afford one or know someone who is; 20th cent: get ticket; bathe, dress in finery, take hackney to concert hall, sit still for hours (no snacking), take hackney home 2. aunt Ethel lives in your village; later: send servant; later: write & post; send telegram 3. houses have only one floor 4. you eat from a communal bowl, have very few dishes, wash by hand; later: lots of dishes & dishpan hands (= unsightly) 5. possess very few clothes, wash in river; later: Tuesday is washday = soak clothes day before, on Tuesday heat wash kettle with wood fire until water boils, dunk and stir and plunger clothes, take out, wring, rinse, wring, rinse, put through hand-cranked wringer, hang on line, take off line, fold & dampen, roll up, iron on Wednesday 6. early: go into the (often wet, cold,) bush; later: build & use (often wet, cold, smelly) outhouse; procure & sprinkle lime/lye 7. get wood, make fire, let burn, open oven door, stick hand in it, if it feels right, put in cake pan with batter, get handkerchief to cry over fallen cake!
turn tap	cold or hot water spouts forth	early: fetch cold H_2O from puddle, pond, stream; later: dig well, build hoist contraption; take bucket, fill, carry back; later: pump in yard, pump with one hand, hold bucket with other. All water is cold.

Magic

We do not feel enchanted. We feel entitled. We take for granted the miracles of modern existence. Becoming blasé is part of our basic make-up. It produces boredom and makes us go forth to think up more magical tricks. To conclude that partial inventory of what we've pulled out of our heads but are no longer amazed by, here are (arguably) the three rabbits most deserving of occasional incredulity: plastic; petroleum-derived clothing; pharmaceuticals.

Pride of place must go to fire as the most magical addition to the lives of humanoids ever. That's why another bit of magic is worth dwelling on: the instant calling forth of a flame with a 2" long sliver of wood. We've long ago stopped to think of the safety match as magical. Yet consider this! The foremother rubs sticks together to get that life-sustaining, fire-starting spark. She muses that there might be an easier way, one not dependent on the fire-spirit, to get and keep fire. She's right; humans are doing very well by banking fires. Embers still glow in the morning, ready to burst into flame. Nomads and tribes moving on learn how to carry glowing cinders over long distances. But it took thousands of years before the fire-spirit finally let go and let us partake in his magic. the match appears in 1830. Those first matches were highly poisonous. The safety match, e.g. non-poisonous, comes on the scene in 1911. Today, other magic notwithstanding, the world lights 500 billion matches a year! Fire at a scratch; instant gratification.

Instant gratification at every scratch, push, turn, flick, swipe, drop, click makes us instantly cross when we are forced to notice that push-button magic does not halt marriage-breakdown, violence, war, unemployment, recessions, and other woes invited by us or visited upon us. Utterly reliant on technological fixes and wonders, we expect—in a subterranean kind of way—the impossible precisely because we don't begin to fathom why or how those labour-saving inventions work. To test our heedless faith in magic, imagine a Person(s)-in-the-Street interview. The following questions are supposed to be answered correctly with an explanation in everyday language of the major steps, processes, or thoughts involved:

- how do all those pictures show up on your tv?
- how does the bank know you rally got no more and no less than two $20 bills + one $10 bill from the ATM after having keyed in a withdrawal of $50.00?
- how exactly is it possible that you can ogle Jenifer Lopez on your computer monitor?
- how does the gas from the pump make the wheels of your car turn?
- where do all those 0s and 1s of the digital age live and how do they cause the system "to do down"?
- how come the Information Age is not called The Knowledge Age or The Age of Wisdom?

No luck, eh? Something weird is going on. The descendants of the veldt people have no idea how most inventions work. Yet some of these same descendants keep inventing and figuring and being brilliant. They make this magic possible. But they don't really know where it's all leading; they just follow their "invent" program, the original "killer app" running in the human brain. What's lately come up is atom-power, cloning, the fax machine, tomatoes with mouse genes

Magic

in them, plastic, laser printers, halogen lights, digital everything, satellite photography, the remote. Yes, it's all magic. And while we use that kind of magic every day, we are using another kind every day as well, talismanic magic. Maybe—since we don't understand the magic that technology and science have wrought—we want to fend off something or other. We still seem to want to propitiate the gods as well as keep lurking malevolent spirits at bay lest the magic desert us.

So we fake a return to "primitive" life. Not that there's anything wrong with that! But the higher tech we get, the more shapeless, crumpled, and indistinct our wearage gets. Even lawyers and bankers adhere to the Friday ritual of the casual costume. It's as if we wanted to go back to a time when we just stumbled out of the cave without having to worry about skirt, hat, pants, tie, shoes! We also re-invent the wheel when we wear crystals, birth stones, "native art", tattoos, "branded" clothing or when we pierce our bodies in visible and invisible regions, can't wait to read our daily horoscope, pay tarot card readers. We also shop for "natural" herbal potions (which contain, thanks to modern extraction technology, rather unnatural amounts of whatever magic substance). Do we hope to fool the hovering evil gremlins into leaving our hi-tech gifts alone because they see us as primitives?

Nor have we evolved away from another "times-past" mode of thinking, the "no pain, no gain" sub-routine. Our collective myths have worn ruts into our brains. There's Prometheus who stole from the gods the magic of fire for the gain of humans. He paid with pain, being chained to a rock for eternity, an eagle plucking at his liver day-in, day-out. To gain heaven for believers, Christ had to suffer the pain of the cross. The gains during seven fat years are inevitably followed by the pain of seven lean ones. Hang around a lotto counter and you'll hear: "I've got it [gain] coming! I've just been through some rough times [pain]!"* And, yes, to gain the land of milk and honey, masses of porridge have to be gulped. The ant works her tiny butt off to keep alive through the winter. We know what happens to that [pain]work-avoiding grasshopper! All myths that explain us to ourselves deal with our species' grumbles about the pain of having to earn our bread by the sweat of the brow.

We know we ought to sweat, so we work out at the fitness centre. We work out until we sweat and our bones ache because that's one way to pay for the good life. (Curiously it's not a "work-out" if one pushes a wheelchair-bound person for a couple of miles every day!) Another way we try to still that unspoken fear that the good fortune of leading such fabulously pampered lives cannot last is by placating those malicious, resentful spirits hovering about. We hope to placate them by making sure they hear that we suffer a wrong or an injustice every five days. We see ourselves as victims. Victims of bureaucracy. Victims of systemic this or that. Victims of fate. Victims of our metabolism. Victims of advertising. We suspect that if we sing in the mornings, we'll have reason to cry at night. So we start the day and find dangers to our health in the enjoyment of crispy

---

* Sometimes "rough times" can be translated as "outlay $120; winnings $0.00".

Magic

bacon, fried eggs, and sugar in our coffee. We are constantly afraid lest mayhem, larceny, or murder befall us even though statistics (which, of course, the devil, the ultimate evil spirit, can quote to his purpose!) show that we have nothing to fear but fear. Watching the nightly parade of "if it bleeds, it leads", temporarily reassures us. *Somebody* out there is suffering. Obviously, the wrathful demons are busy elsewhere and our charmed lives are safe for the moment.

When next time you work off that banana fritter[*] on the electrically powered tread-mill in the air-conditioned fitness club to which you've driven while your programmed VCR records an event which takes place 8,300 km away, be sure to finger your most recently purchased worry-beads with that hand attached to the copper bracelet-encircled wrist. You want to keep the universe unfolding as it should!

---

[*] the banana being, magically, a standard food item in the non-tropical zone where you live

SAINTS

> The blue and white racing suit worn by Elvis Presley in the 1968 movie *Speedway* fetched nearly $16,365 ... . But they lost out on Elvis's midnight blue velvet shirt, bought by British comedian Frank Skinner for $18,000. "Everyone should have a bit of Elvis in their lives," Skinner said.
>
> News Item

To own the very thing which touched a celebrity or revered person seems a deeply compelling desire in humans. To have the "thing" stand for the personage started with our far-off ancestors. They put through their noses or hung around their necks a bone, a tooth, a claw of an admired animal. Later along the timeline, our great-grandparents[~4] enshrined body parts of sainted persons, carried around with them an item said to have belonged to them, or gave a place of honour to their iconic images in whatever dwelling. Our age carries on, wanting to possess what the famous have worn, played with, driven. At the bottom of this seemingly irrational behaviour lies the urge to survive, an urge well served by looking to those who visibly survive and survive well. They serve us as exemplar. We seem born with the unspoken assumption that if our hand touches the successful entity, some of their success may rub off on us.

The celebrity cult of our time is built upon the adoration of the churched saints which, in turn, had its origin in the veneration of animals and those humans who excelled at hunting them down. At one point our clever brains transferred the significance we gave to the hero-animal or hero-human to a representation: a painting on a cave wall. That morphed into an illumination in a manuscript which became the photo in a glossy magazine. Today images of the celebrated in moments sublime as well as ridiculous are reproduced millions[*] of times. Anyone who packages and markets the images, lives, or leavings of the famous will not die a pauper. If we want to own an item associated with the admired entity, we show faith in enhancement-by-association, something that has had our entire collective past to become ingrained.

In that far off time the "to do list" of the day had only one item on it: "get food". We know that something like a ✓ mark would be in order after finding a few roots, birds' eggs, or fruit. The procurement of concentrated protein in the form of meat, however, must have warranted ✓ ✓ ✓ even though we had no idea that meat-eating would enlarge our collective brain to the extent that it would invent instant coffee, French fries, even soy hamburger-"meat". This most desirable [brain] food came on the hoof. A whole lot of animal—meat to feast on for days, large pieces of fur, a supply of bones handy as tools or shelter material—was worth its weight. There we have it: the concept of "worth". The animal is worth the hunt and putting one's entire resources into it. The hunter admires the worthy adversary, its cunning, its speed, its strength. Once brought down, the hunter takes a claw, a tooth, a tuft of hair to hang around his

---

[*] The *National Enquirer* all by itself accounts for almost 3,000,000 copies

neck, thereby to partake of the animal's virtues. The body part is on its way to become talisman, trophy, relic.

What we call a "role model" today was, in a manner of speaking, invented by the hunter-gatherers. The tribe assigned worthiness to the most accomplished hunter, the most expert gatherer. They would be looked up to, if not venerated, because life depended on what the hunter managed to kill and what the gatherer managed to find. That member of the tribe most fleet of foot, strong of arm, courageous of deed became the role model for the hunter. The gatherers might look up to a woman who had gained distinction because she could always discover birds' nests or find fat roots where others could not. As well she'd think up a new way to preserve a strip of fish. Comeliness as the sole characteristic would not have gone unremarked or unenvied. Some children may have harboured the wish to succeed the healer, that person who could find, identify, and use herbs, grasses, flowers, bark, roots, seeds with which to perform near miracles. Being better at something meant not only living better; it also meant being admired, maybe even famous.[*]

Time passes; the culture changes. Because culture gives expression to our basic wiring by means of the tools/technology invented during a particular era, a fast forward from pre-historic to agricultural times shows us quite a different hero/ine: the Saint. Admiration for physical

---

[*] However, being famous merely for being famous is a newly sprouted, luxuriantly growing sapling from that old trunk of animal worship.

prowess shifts to veneration of a life lived virtuously. Veneration of the noble beast battling the brave hunter before being vanquished by him—and the spilling of blood—shifts to idolization of the suffering endured by humans (often flowing blood being in evidence as well). The cult of the martyr arises in which the emphasis is put on the suffering of excruciating torture, followed by a gruesome death, rather than on the virtuous life she/he had lived.

The martyrs' goodness and unshakability of faith, for which they had to suffer grievously, was taken for granted. Often it is the tormented death which compels the adoring public to procure anything from the body of a sainted human: a heart, skull, tooth, a bone splinter, a lock of hair. Brisk demand develops for bits of the machinery employed to bring virtue to its knees: a piece of the cross, a snippet of the whip, a spike from the rack. No less desired are threads and patches from the dress worn by the sufferer. These relics are enshrined and displayed in places of worship. For every-day use, but cherished just the same, is the slip of parchment with a saint's approximate likeness drawn upon it.

The saint industry was born. The iconic image was something real to have and to hold, something which stood for an abstraction—virtue. But abstractions are not really our forte. Soon, if not indeed right from the start, the iconic image stood for the narrative of a life. Humans don't identify with ideas or events; we identify with that which provides the bedrock of gossip, the details of another person's life. The stuff of tales in those medieval TV-bereft evenings, the subject matter of the actors' performance in the midst of the twice-yearly market, the most entertaining part during the church sermon was the narration of a life, taken from a best-seller of the times, *Lives of the Saints*.

Our proclivity to look to a life more extraordinary than ours, in whatever aspect, remains unchanged. What has changed is the sheer amount of hagiology out there. The "saint" industry of our age has taken on truly staggering proportions. Veritable legions of magazines are devoted to one theme only, the comings, goings, and taking breath of the breath-takingly beautiful, successful, or merely notorious. As ever, a good living can be made by those who supply what the multitudes crave.

Today's hunters, having bagged their prey with a camera mounted to the photographer's shaft, offer their kill to those who can make useable items of the haul. Many "items" will then be disgorged by the teller of the tale, sitting by our fire, television. This 24/7 open maw disgorges a steady pixel stream of intimate portraits, biographies, lives dramatized, lives mini-seried, lives two-hour-specialled. Then we get the (R)epeats! Television and the Internet, technologies that do not require reading, offer the celebrity as interviewer, interviewee, talk-show host, game show contestant, event or colour commentator. Most often celebrity status arises in the first place from playing, that is, representing someone else's life in a moving picture narrative. Hi-tech makes the pictures, pictures which, by the way, had to be made by our brain in the cave days of the storyteller.

Saints

That story, a figment of the imagination, remains the same but is now enhanced with the highest tech we're capable of. The moving picture was "invented" by that same brain that came up with the idea to take some coloured clay, add some fluid, dip fingers in it, and then draw upon the wall of a dwelling the pictures in the mind. And right from the start what was painted was that which was most admired: the strongest, the swiftest, the most courageous and powerful animals. (Humans had to wait a few hundred years to see their likeness.)[*] We so much take for granted the daily glut of visual images that we give no thought to that first time when hunter, animal, weapon, speed, exertion, adrenaline-rush got all rolled into one emotion and given expression by fixing it upon a surface.

The desire to behold—and behold repeatedly, at will, in one's own time and space—the likeness of the admired moved from the cave wall to the church wall to a piece of parchment to the page of a tabloid. The picture is, and always was, worth a thousand words.[†] During the Middle Ages the burgeoning country and town life increased the numbers of the faithful. The Church beatified the martyr, the missionary, the staunch defender of the faith. Fame of saintly behaviour spread far and wide via itinerant monks, sermons, morality plays. The saints now served as role models. Their exemplary lives were held up to be imitated

---

[*] This happened about 17,000 years, or 850 generation, ago. (Reminder: since our calendar year zero, only 100 generations have told their stories.)

[†] Knowing that we hold a digitally modified photo will not change the neurology that "gets the picture" in a fraction of the time it would take to describe in words—printed or spoken—what's on it.

as best one could. But it was not the prescriptive part of the uplifting tale that mesmerized the devout, it was the irresistible entertainment value—as we know only too well—of the ingenious violence and gruesome killing contained in that very tale.

Warning! This paragraph contains images which may be disturbing to some readers. Nevertheless, it is recommended reading for those who beat their breast and rend their clothes crying that never was entertainment as gruesome as it is today. What was the high point in many a saint's life was their death. The end of a sainted life was more often than not accompanied by intense suffering inflicted by innovative torture leading to a degrading as well as grisly death. Under its veneer of edification, this entertainment could be found painted in panels inside churches, set in stained glass, carved in wood, or sculpted in marble. St. Bartholomew dripped blood as his tormentor, wielding a knife as if skinning a rabbit, flayed the martyr alive. Tied to a huge spiked wheel, made to revolve slowly by human arms, St. Katherine was made to inch in agony toward her death.[*] St. Simon's body parts could be seen lying about him as his executioner re-positioned a hand-saw to dismember him further until he breathed his last. The greatest mental as well as physical suffering is displayed to this day along one of the walls in Catholic churches all over the world. Often painted by local artisans, they depict the Fourteen Stations of the Cross. Each panel shows another "instalment" in the story of Christ's hideous torture and death.   The faithful are asked to

---

[*] In the end St. Katherine's life was spared through divine intervention.

contemplate each station for the length of time it takes to say one rosary. Quentin Tarantino, eat your heart out!

Gazing upon the spectacle of suffering brings forth in us fascination and horror; we identify with that other human being. The ancient Greeks talked of tragedy—character, circumstance, and fate coming together to cause a catastrophe to befall a powerful person—arousing pity and fear. These emotions of pity and fear were then thought to be purged in the audience after they had watched a tragedy unfold. Sort of fighting fire with fire. The cathartic moment comes also, no doubt, when we weigh our rather insignificant troubles against those endured by the famous, the powerful, the great, the blameless, the virtuous, or the holy. It follows that the contemplation of suffering provides comfort and solace and has done so for ever. And does so today.

Elizabeth Taylor's suffering, her "14 stations of the cross", illustrated with photos taken at the various milestones in her life, given short captions supplying data, published in 18 million tabloids—and repeated and repeated, year after year, in diverse publications—satisfies, at bottom, the same need to seek comfort in the calamities of others.[*] And since, as we have seen, fame and frisson create a market for bits of anything that has intimately touched the legendary human,

---

[*] We obey, or try to obey, the saint's admonitions. Elizabeth Taylor's endorsements have been powerfully profitable in very disparate ventures: her fund-raising for the battle against AIDS and the marketing of her line of perfume.

Saints

we too line up to offer what is required to get a piece of those who entertain as well as comfort us in our time.

For tens of thousands of years we revered powerful animals, knew intimately their habits, and treasured some thing that signified their identity. For almost two thousand years we revered virtuous humans, knew every story in the *Lives of the Saints*, and treasured some thing that had been part of them. For less than 100 years we have celebrated lives—or "life styles" in the parlance of the now—of humans who have been shone upon not by the sun, not by a god, but by the limelight, our very own invention. The dark recesses of the caves needed a torch to illuminate the drawings of the animal and, later, that of the bleeding, dying hunter. The dark churches of the immediate past needed the light of votive candles to illuminate the icons of the saints, the halo of the burning wick transferred to the saint's head. The hi-tech age provides the glare of the limelight, the flash of the camera, the klieglight of the movie studio to produce the icons we behold in the darkness of the living room or the multiplex.

In that bright spot surrounded by darkness, the animal, the saint, the celebrity offers never-ending subject matter: fact, fancy, conjecture, tidbits, hearsay, eye-witness accounts, personal observations, data ... in short, whatever we have revered, we have been able to gossip about. As soon as technology made it possible, the gossip industry kicked into high gear to satisfy an insatiable demand. We buy posters of our "saints". We buy books about and by them. We flock to the sound-bites of *Entertainment Tonight*. We drive all the

way to the mall when one of today's saints does a promo.
We buy what they buy (or say they buy); we holiday where
they live; we bid for their cast-offs; we celebrate by eating in
restaurants in which they have a stake; we name our children
after them. We care about their parents, their children, their
dogs. We want to know their dress size, their favourite
drink, whether they dye their hair or not.

> "TV Guide reports that crew members filled up
> jugs of water from the Melrose pool, the site of
> much cavorting among the show's characters.
> Fox [Network] plans to fill hundreds of plastic
> vials for eventual distribution to fans."
>
> News item (April 24, 1999)

Each age seems to have the saints, heroes, and the merely
notorious that the concurrent technology produces and, in a
way, demands. The hunter venerated the animal he
depended on and the best of his own species. The tiller of
the soil prayed to those who led admirable lives and
postponed gratification to be assured life everlasting.
Industrial man looked to the Horatio Alger mold: orderly,
frugal, hard-working, inventive, quick-thinking, willing to
struggle. Until the first stirrings of the electronic age after
the Second World War, the role model tended to be
overwhelmingly a human being who placed—or seemed to
place—the social good, the community, and the adherence to
a set of rules of behaviour above their own interests.

Now, in hi-tech times, with the attendant life of ease—the
never-befores of the 24/7 open food gathering places, the 3
T-shirts @ $12.99, instant assistance by pressing 911, fast

pain relief, paved streets—we need neither strength, virtue, nor 60-hour work weeks to survive. We can afford the money and the time to indulge our appetite for gossipy minutiae of other people's lives. Despite myriad offerings by the mass media and other modern distractions, the fascination with the lives of those who have achieved 15 minutes or 2 hours or x years of fame persists. Although 96% of all teenagers in our culture can not name even one saint, 96% of all teenagers can ream off their "fave's" preference in clothes, food, work-out routines, pets, cars, dates, hobbies, music, flowers, colours. They would kill for a scrap of wearage—deemed to be authentic—cast off by their idol of the moment.

And it's not only teenagers. Even if we post-twenty year olds don't model ourselves after this or that famous person, their very fame induces us to want to know more about how they live, what they think, how they speak, what their goals are. Older members of the tribe, who fancy themselves above frenzied worship, spend the time they have (and often time they do not have) on what is, basically, gossip. Without spinning that gossip into one hell of a long yarn, the hard facts of the O. J. Simpson trial, John Kennedy Jr.'s death, or the Clinton-Lewinsky affair would not have filled more than 3 minutes of daily air-time. The TV-commercial-biz loves us gossip junkies. Serials about any kind of person(s) create devotees within a definable demographic and in measurable numbers. Bookstores' bottom lines are not imperiled by stocking an abundance of definitive and not so definitive biographies of the famous. There's even a brisk trade in that astonishing consumer item, the autobiography (giving gainful employment to writers whose names appear after the "As told to ...") which appears on the shelf before the celebrity has reached half of her/his life expectancy.

Yet, even a life lived only to its mid-point stokes our fascination with the tribulations visited upon its celebrated span. We get the same goosebumps as did our ancestors when they beheld the vicissitudes, the persecutions, and ultimate martyrdom of the saints. Today's celebrities suffer their demons. They are tortured—and we are properly mesmerized by the incongruity—either by, or despite of, the availability of money, opportunity, and vast acclaim. They are beset by the demons of alcohol misuse, drug addiction, out-of-control tempers, indiscriminate and copious coupling, egos larger than their multi-million dollar houses. It looks as if at any minute the coach might turn into the pumpkin ... and we might get to watch it!

A helping of torture and misery endured by someone famous is our favourite (self)indulgence. As the saints were tortured and put to death for their beliefs, so today's famous are tormented and made wretched by their very celebrity status and riches. The personage par excellence in the modern panoply of The Sainted was surely Princess Diana. Beautiful, wealthy, a princess, publicly displaying the various (emotional) wounds inflicted by the 20th century equivalent of the torturer, she was finally being sacrificed on the altar built to our current obsession with wanting to possess "a piece of" a saint. Armies of paparazzi pursued her so her devotees could behold her likeness on a piece of paper or in a TV newsclip. That, at least, is the narrative.

Saints

These being fast-moving times, however, the waves of adulation receded soon after this particular saint's demise.

Diana's trajectory, nevertheless, serves to illustrate that in each saint's life something unexpectedly or astonishingly bad must occur. It does not matter whether the ultimate catastrophe is caused by a character flaw or an outside event or a fateful coming together of both. It will never do to lead merely a "good" life; a blameless life lacks the necessary drama to keep us fascinated. (Of course, we are charmed by a token community-minded saint occasionally. Mother Teresa comes to mind.) We must exclaim—or at least subconsciously come to the conclusion—that our lives are not so bad after all when compared to the suffering of the great, rich, famous, saintly. We want their lives to be more charmed than our own; at the same time we need to see that they too suffer. It's that sweet and irrational human thing again: wanting to eat the cake while hanging on to it.

We want the drama (the cake) but drama presupposes suffering, occasionally even death (the demise of the cake). Absolutely everyone suffers at some time or another, Linda more than Beverly, David less than Kyle. But going through a bad stretch, suffering, hurting is—we don't just say it; we know it in our bones—relative. We also know that those who feel wounded **are** wounded. Our comfort is to read and see that even saints and stars suffer, suffer more grievously than we do. They fall lower because they stood higher. We are linked to the Great Admired Ones through our suffering on the one hand; on the other we are placated since not even riches, greatness, or advantage provide a shield against adversity.

The literal shield against adversity is the iconic representation. In cave-days it was an amulet carved vaguely in the shape of an animal; in knight-days it was the holy picture. Saint Barbara, despite a stereotypical face, was recognized instantly because a halo surrounded her head. A tower—famously associated with her life and fate—could also always be seen in the picture somewhere. In instant-replication-days the real face of the celebrity, every pore of it, is shown over and over and over, until it becomes as iconic as that icon of St. Barbara. In our minds, a thumbnailed individuality, a mini-narrative, attaches itself to the image.

And the image is every bit as meaningful to us as was the saint's picture on the church wall to past generations. Our poster saints, found in thousands of bedrooms, rec rooms, dens, shacks, office cubicles, workshops, are chosen for one distinctive attribute. Farah Fawcett's mane signals the adventuresome hi-jinks of *Charlie's Angels*, Marlon Brando's sulk & sneer suggests uncluttered male virility, and Shania Twain's belly-button advertises the abs-über-alles sexiness of today. Our icons are not only associated with the events in their real lives but also with their lives on screen. Tom Cruise, much idolized for his good looks, dazzling smile, and body language of the semi-shy, is the poster boy for male teens who wish they'd look like him, smile like him. Themselves in a shy and awkward state, they yearn for the "cool" way he manages events in the movie life of his greatest successes, *Risky Business*, *Top Gun*, *Mission Impossible*. During those nano-seconds that it takes us to recognize that unmistakable face, our brains reel off a montage of the icon's real and virtual life. All of which is big business: Tom Cruise can command, and get, $27 million per movie; Tom Cruise will be worth every penny to his owners, be they the studio execs or the cine-plex public.

> Although the rubies on them aren't real, the red pumps made for Judy Garland to dance in *The Wizard of Oz* fetched $666,000 in an auction. The new owner considers the shoes "the Holy Grail" of film props.
>
> From a news item [People, 6/12/00]

The hypester and the consumer alike talk about their idols in the language of a waning religion. It's the same as borrowing the terms of the previous technology for our new inventions. We express the power of the car in terms of what horses can do; we see a desktop on our computer screen; we deliver our voice into a telephone mail-box. Today's ubiquitous word "icon" meant, only 30 years ago, a representation of some sacred personage, the icon itself being also venerated. The paradigmatic icon of our time, Oprah, is described with words and phrases befitting any saint of yore. Because they so convincingly buttress the gist of this chapter, some quotes from *US weekly*[*] (June 12, 2000) and its *Special Report on Oprah*.

---

[*] The play on "US" conveys in two letters what this chapter has taken many hundreds of words to illustrate: what's between the covers on a weekly basis is "us".

Saints

The *Special Report* introduces "The High Priestess of Positivity". Applause she receives is "ecstatic". She is no less than a "bona fide icon" and has been called "a source of wonder", "a wonder maker". A recipient of Oprah's bounteousness (which is one of the virtues of a saint) tells her child: "`When you want change, pray to St. Oprah`". During a party our modern saint is said to have "shone her light on everyone", have people "follow this woman all the way to an A+", "convincing millions of Americans" of her approach to life. Oprah's rise from being born poor, black, a woman is called "a trinity of daunting obstacles that gives her triumph an almost biblical resonance". This "authentic folk figure" is "soulful, pious, wise". This is a description of a modern role-model which would have, phrase for phrase, done a 12th century, pope-sanctioned saint proud!

The remainder of the hagiographic piece contains the obligatory reference to a saint's demons, in this case Oprah's love of food and her struggles to keep her weight down. She battles temptation because, like the saints of other times, "[s]he's not perfect but she wants to be". The saint of self-improvement is doing what saints have always done: tell & show. Oprah, who "as a child dreamed of becoming a missionary, who has always referred to her show as a `ministry`", is the preacher-saint. For day-time worship her sermons regularly pack the highest number of television faithful into the pews.

The interdependence of The Life and the representational, fixed image holds true for this modern saint as well. The article, *Oprah's World,* features, cover image included, six pictures and two (2) "Stations in the Life" montages. One of these is a series of eight panels, each displaying the icon Oprah chronologically from 1984 to 2000. The other one is an arrangement of circular snapshots documenting her "evolution" from star to icon. The composition of these round photos, covering the entire page, is oddly reminiscent of the stained glass window. Helpfully it's made clear, without quite stooping, what an icon is today. "She's one of the few human beings on the planet immediately identifiable to hundreds of millions of people by her first name alone. Her face is as recognizable as that of any ... religious leader." And this in "200 U.S. markets and about 140 international ones." In the U.S. alone, 33 million people come to her every week.

Pay homage to Icon Oprah every day in many ways: watch her talk-show, buy a tabloid, subscribe to her *O* magazine, pay for a book she has read and recommends, cook with her recipe book, rent a video with her in the movie's starring role, go on her diet. The Oprah industry is the saint industry but exponentially enhanced by the latest technology. Clutching a magazine with Oprah on the cover and the self-improvement road to temporal salvation promised inside, we figuratively touch the hem of the great celebrated personage. From this warm feeling of adulation it's only a step to the desire to own that hem because it touched the adored.

Role models come in many shapes; we've seen them morph from animal to saint to celebrity. Shakespeare expressed best that we follow a script when he said: "All the world's a stage, and all the men and women merely players" (*As You*

Like It). And it so happens that our scripts are made up of every triumph savoured, every vicissitude endured by the great. Above all, we want to know every tiny happening in their every waking moment so that we can find vague parallels to our own lives. The significance in the one lends importance to the other. The role model serves as *The Book of Instructions How To Cope with Life*. That "book" is condensed into the icon. The perceived strengths and virtues of the admired animal or saint seep to one's self from a bone, a hair, a picture. This is good survival behaviour. Homo sapiens has benefited from looking to guidelines for eons. Those who follow a recipe bake a better cake.

PRINT IS TOAST

> "Print is toast!"
> Bruce Willis, actor and
> celebrity (Cannes 1998)

Scientific proof does not exist that reading and comprehending one hundred and forty eight words of printed text[*] comes easily to all human beings. We can be taught to decipher the black marks on the page but—as with any other taught skill—some of us will barely manage, some will become adequate, some will excel. Knowing how to read has to be learned. Knowing how to look comes with us at birth as a built-in feature. And, as successful technology tends to do, the one now meshing (*pace* those who think "messing" would better describe the situation!) with our synapses blinks, whirrs, and clicks into something that's been there, although rudimentary, since fishes came on the scene. We respond well to the global high-tech information culture because it fits into the habit world of the hunter-gatherer tribe: the intake of information by looking, talking, listening.

Most information already comes by look instead of by book. Because Marshall McLuhan's "the global village" and "the medium is the message" have been sound-bites for so long, it's become axiomatic that how we get our information determines the kind of culture we live in. By getting our information more and more from visuals all around us and

---

[*] the number of words in this paragraph, for example

less and less from thousands of lines of print squeezed into a book, we are letting the hunter-gatherer in us determine today's and, so it seems, the immediate future's culture.

Ever since we became large-brained, we have looked for information: about a never seen before root, a way to improve a tool, where to find new pasture. Looking for and finding and passing on information is the life-blood of our species. That we found a way to encode it and pass it along has increased our numbers to 6.1 billion info gobblers. Print, as an information carrier, packs a wallop: it's easily produced and reproduced, secure from tampering, portable, lasting, and holds still for rapid or slow intake. However, during those 40,000 years since Cro-Magnon transmitted data, readily reproduced print has been with us for only the last 400.

For our essentially still stone-age physiology, it's not a good fit to get information in print mode. It's easy to look and talk; it's hard to learn to read and write. We're evolved to function in a collection of people who share a relatively small space, mostly stay put, know each other by name, are kin to half the folk in the tribe, are guided by the same beliefs, do some tilling, gathering, hunting. This was, by and large, village life as well. In that setting one's brain was not asked to train the eye along lines made up of variously shaped marks; instead information got picked from a bunch of visual clues. Now it so happens that our latest brainchild, the globe-conquering digital processor, scatters over our information-rich landscape congenial visual clues: icons here; icons there; icons simply everywhere.

Print is Toast

That processor[*] enjoys such all-embracing success with us humans because it lets us look again, lets our eye randomly surf instead of forcing it to move along straight lines and from line to line. Click the mouse-button or touch the screen and look at a world of information effortlessly wherever you are. And since the hankering to get with the program, to partake in that information gusher is world-wide, one can assume that print has never really "taken". A *print*-culture did exist for about 300 years. During that time the truly literate tended not only to set the tone in their society; they judged "what is and is not done". They reigned over high culture; they reigned in church, government, and factory. They reigned because they could get at, possess, and use most or all information that was available.

The print-oriented brains ran things. The print-maven drove the culture. Which is why we talk of a print-culture. That is not the same as having everyone print-enculturated. When Bruce Willis said "Print is toast", he referred to the print-culture as those born before 1950 knew it. Print will be used in the information age but it will not rule. There will still be the printing of letters, jotting down of notations, or reading of short captions. We will not see the demise of: "2:40 drive Tommy to dentist", "Tiger blooms with another 64 Desert Classic", "8 unread messages", "Take 2 tablets every 3 hours", or "hi hotlipps were your from". What will be gone

---

[*] It's so spookily like our brain that really smart persons are called "brainiacs", presumably because they very much resemble that granddad of computers, the ENIAC (Electronic Numerical Integrator And Calculator, 1946-1955). Of course, we invented it; it has to work like our brain does.

Print is Toast

is a culture that took its ideas, its ethics, its role models, its aesthetic, its way of life from books and passed that way of life on to the next generation, again mostly through the authority of the written word.

All new technologies start out by aping the old. Each new technology transforms the previous one into something faster, higher, wider, more efficient, more fun. The four wheels on the car imitated those four already familiar from the ox-cart; the inspiration for those four wheels came, no doubt, from the four legs of the pack-animal. One can look at the gestation of the computer in the same way. Initially the computer was a powerful and rapid calculator and nothing else. In this it followed the evolution of writing. Numerals—in the form of notches—for recording quantity came before letters denoting words. In the same way the spread-sheet was the first killer-application; the word-processor came second ... and quite a bit later. The first promised to make everyone into a successful business person. It made possible a kind of dance of the figures which revealed within seconds a "if this, then that" scenario for bottom-line aficionados. The second promised to transform everyone into a writer because, so we naively believed, one could turn out flawless-looking copy.

However, to become an excellent, or merely proficient, bottom-liner or writer, one had to have a head for abstractions and a liking for black marks on a white background. We were still in print-culture land. This newest tool, at that moment, could be wielded with competence only by a relative few in the human tribe (this would have been so even if every single person on the globe had been issued with the necessary gear). For a while it seemed that competence with a computer would just be another form of being literate. Soon, however, more people than ever before—people who had never crossed the threshold of a library, people who had no books in their homes, people who neither wrote nor got personal letters— were able to get at information by using a computer.

The ultimate killer-app had arrived! Everyone can handle the browser; everyone can roam the Internet; everyone can look, should they be so inclined, at the collected information-trove of the global tribe. More pictures than print; icons instead of print commands; gorgeous 256+ colours, animation, cartoons, charts, film clips, sounds, video, and NEWS in moving pictures; the whole world is but a mouse-click and a glimpse-look away.

What rivets us to that monitor is that no matter what, our brains get information directly, without the interposition of something that first needs deciphering. Mostly what we see is something new. And we crave news, that is, change. New song, new dress, new schedule, new recipe, new CEO, new partner, new pepper mill. News is anything that changes the status quo. News is information; information is news. Craving, ingesting, and digesting news is only a smidgen away in importance from craving, ingesting, and digesting food. Once, when we hunted, news of where a bunch of deer roamed was prized. So was the information that strips of fish, slowly dried in the sun, will keep until the next snow has fallen and melted. Sharing news about food is basic wiring. Bees do it; they fly in a particular pattern to direct their mates to a specific pollen find. Birds do it; throw a few crumbs around in a forest clearing and be amazed by what comes out of the woodwork. Human's mouse-click is about getting a fundamental need fulfilled more easily, more quickly, more pleasurably than plodding through print on a page.

The word "information" is synonymous with the word "news". The appearance of a new tool must have been considered important new(s) information already in the stone age. Although a mite removed from flint-stone chipping times, we are as eager as ever to hear about, or look at, anything new that other humans come up with. Today news about the latest tool in whatever branch of human endeavour spreads with the speed of the zinging electron. Immediately almost every member of the global tribe aches to possess what the high-technology tool shapers and digital program coders have wrought.

We **must** have the newest tools because from the paleolithic dawn onward those who cut chips more ingeniously from the flint stone had the more efficient tool. They hunted better, lived better, could feed more off-spring to adulthood. Somewhere along the timeline, the alpha chippers lived very well because they had the equivalent of "coin" in hand. This decent supply of currency they received for the newest, "technologically enhanced" hand axe. And so did, of course, those who had the wit to see that the new and improved stone scraper could clean a hide more easily and faster.

Print is Toast

People will talk about this "news" and spread new-tool information. Getting information about a new tool and wanting to posses it are a hair's width apart. Looking at a representation of a new tool (or toy) is the most congenial for our stone-age[*] information processors. Hearing about something new from a trusted source—word-of-mouth advertising, really—comes second in effectiveness. But even the most handsomely laid-out lines of print are only third-best in attracting our attention and our wish to care about that new (maybe income enhancing) artifact.

More on news ... when we encounter a newsy item, good or bad, we do tingle with a thrill. News is valuable in that it may add a wrinkle to one's ability to make a (better) living. News can cause us cry, calm down, confabulate, celebrate, commit suicide. News is invaluable as a reason to make our "have you heard?" bonding visits or phone calls to persons who are kin by virtue of shared blood, hobby, or social set. The itch to tell others of an event that just happened or is still happening is a trigger from long ago as well. Despite all-news channels, despite news up-dates during regular radio and TV programs, despite the certain head-line in tomorrow's paper, phone lines will be tied up when "news" happens (Kennedy; Challenger; Diana ... & those are just the biggies!; for local flavour add a fire, an earth tremor, a power outage).

We've always tried to cast as broadly as possible whatever information we deem news. The smoke signal, the bush bongo, the town crier, the postal pony, the Morse code, all

---

[*] The Bronze age lies only about 300 generations back.

had their day in the sun. All these info transmitters served our passion for news. We got to know that an enemy was approaching, a friendly band needed help, a new chief had been elected[*], a personage had died, that little Luke had been born, that the Titanic was in distress. None of those message carriers were ever devised to convey the idea of the categorical imperative or the fact that the square of the hypotenuse of a right triangle is equal to the sum of the squares of the other sides. News is what we can sop up without strain while chewing a betel nut. News deals with what's real. CNN and its other 24/7 cousins achieve a pleasing bottom line because they wouldn't dream of showing a discussion about the compositional merits of atonal music.

Despite the conquest of popular culture over high-brow culture, neither philosophy nor geometry nor talking about music will disappear. But the tube—or its Internet equivalent—is not the right place for abstractions. We click on the remote or an icon to get our information as we did 10,000 and more years ago, by looking.[†] And, judging by the trouncing TV and other IT[‡] have given the book, looking

---

[*] The Vatican to this day announces the election of a new pope by sending smoke up a chimney to convey the news to the assembled multitudes in St. Peter's Square.

[†] This kind of "looking" is not the same as looking at a printed page

[‡] The Neanderthals made short grunty, but meaningful, noises. Our passion for the use of abbreviations may not necessarily signal sophistication. TV is part of our grunt repertoire; IT (information technology) will soon join TV.

is not only easier on the brain, it's a lot more fun.[*] Watching and becoming familiar with images from all over the world has made us, as Marshall McLuhan predicted, into village folk. Print culture did not take hold globally, and it is dying where once it reigned successfully. Print's culture-shaping influence has not spread everywhere although for a few seconds of geological time it was assumed that it would.

In contrast, the click & look, search-engine-found, thumb-nail-sketch information circles and cycles through the global village as speedily as any news ever did within a hamlet. This information-sharing, however superficial that "sharing" may be, does give us the feeling that we belong to one tribe rather than to one in the midst of many others which we do not, nor care to, understand. Besides, we looked at our common home on TV: planet earth photographed from afar. We look at this ball much as a Cro-Magnon would look down on her piece of sustaining territory or a medieval peasant on his village if only they went a distance and climbed high enough. The feeling of belonging is the same.

The hi-tech sector of our tribe that figured out how to get a camera far enough into space so it could peer back at the place it came from is frenetically breeding picture-catchers and picture-dispensers. Their various upgrades and newgrades hit the market by the week. In this particular domain just about every invention allows us to act and react as we did in tribal and village times because we can **see**

---

[*] Per day: average TV watching 2.2 hours; average reading ½ hour. (As a wag observed, how much of that ½ hour goes to "reading" the TV schedule?)

what's happening. For instance, instead of having to look
with the naked eye where the horse is going with us (and the
buggy), we look at a GPS navigation screen on the dash of
our many-horses-powered car. In either case we're basically
looking at a picture.

That we now see rather than read what's happening is "the
son of print". The offspring, today's and presumably the
immediate future's technology, uses zeros and ones as
building blocks. It guides our return to a pre-print world we
never entirely left, that is, never evolved beyond. What is
curious about our enthusiastic drift[*] toward and into the
global village is that it is print, with its extremely linear and
sequential shoe-horning of our thinking, that led within a
mere 500-year span rather rapidly to the ultimate abstraction
and the ultimate reduction:
> · the total "order" of the digital revolution
> · the DNA sequencing of the Human Genome Project.

What's more orderly and more abstract than a linear
succession of zeros and ones? 1111101000 is binary code
for 1000. What's more reductive than to undertake a project
which will tell each and every one of us what, if not indeed
who, we are? Despite its 3 billion base pairs (on the 23
chromosomes in each cell), DNA codes with only four
letters: ATCG = **A**denine, **T**hymine, **C**ytosine, and **G**uanine.
Here it is in its stunning simplicity/complexity: human code
= 4 letters; computer code = one cipher, one stroke. Thank

---

[*] The word "drift" has been chosen on purpose since we did not, either
as a collective or as a singleton, lie sleepless at night planning a return to
our roots.

goodness Star Trek's Dr. Spock prepared us to understand that there is "infinite diversity in infinite combinations"!

At this point it's just as well to bring up the fact that binary or gene coding or de-coding is extremely hard, if not impossible, for most of us. For a great number of people reading is just as difficult. It behooves the print-oriented ones, born to the page, to cease taking themselves as the measure of all things. However, they shall be forgiven for they do not know just how hard reading is. It's not enough to look at the printed page; those lines have to be translated. For the translating one has to know what each of 26 symbols stands for, then make out what each small strung-together symbol-combination means, all the while one must keep in mind what the previous bunch of ever varying combos conveyed, then advance, and repeat the process. At intervals—and if one wants to "translate" fluently—a kind of picture has to have formed in one's mind. That's one heck of a round-about way to get at information. Deciphering print is artificial in that the lines upon lines do not make sense as easily to our brains as do ready-made pictures, visuals. The decoding requires effort, has to be school-taught, and is more easily learned by some than by others. Inspirational anecdotes to the contrary, many humans can no more be taught to read with ease than they can be told to change the colour of their eyes.

Our default setting happens to be *looking* at what is— without the brain having to "translate" from an abstraction (often even translating an abstraction, the word, into another abstraction, e.g. *justice, imperative, time & space & matter*).

Print is Toast

For rapid and survival enhancing information-intake our first impulse is to look, to listen, and to talk. If this seems obvious to the point of the reader's eyes rolling upward … good! Then none of us will have any trouble understanding our headlong rush to the place we never really left: the hunter-gatherer habitat.

We homo sapiens sapiens have been around for roughly 130,000 years. Only 400 of those (and that's being generous since not everyone could read even only 150 years ago … nor can today) was spent in a "did you read …?" culture. Already we're well on the way back into a "did you see …?" culture. We are sloughing off the looking at lines of marks representing sounds representing words representing real life. Ideas, spinnings of the mind, are abstractions presented via abstractions. (That's why Philosophy 406 has only a handful of students; they have to **read** Plato's very words. At the 400 level *Coles'* Notes won't do.)

Print has been already demoted from major domo to entry-level servant. It serves by holding the door so we may enter a virtually real world. From e-mail to chat-rooms to URLs, filling in contest-forms or buying pre-printed greeting cards, agonizing through multiple choice tests to punching addresses into a PDA, when do we really write? Yes, we do make things-to-do lists and scribble supermarket items on the back of envelopes (on envelopes, one might add, that brought word-processed, mail-merged hustle letter trying to pry funds from 5,326 others on a scannable, clickable data record). The eye → brain appeal of the pictorial is the return to the future.

Print is Toast

Reading and writing will become, even more than it has been hitherto, the specialty of only a few pods inside the www. Voice-recognition by our electronic pals is just down the road a bit. At that point not even the rudimentary keyboarding, letter-for-letter, to e-mail, chat in chat-rooms, post to x.alt., draft proposals, up-date the day-timer will be needed. E-mail, initially hailed as the saviour of the art and joy of (letter)writing, will keep its name but not its keyboarding. Besides, in the wireless universe it would be too time-consuming to key a proper letter into the button pad of the cell-phone. Voice-recognition is the next step in updating our arrowheads into the universal tool. In a global economy what appeals universally sells. For sharing information voice recognition—also known as talking & listening—came long, long before print recognition.

Icon-selection and voice-recognition are the equivalent of looking, talking, listening during tribal-life times. Any normal[*] person would sufficiently be in command of these basic information tools to ensure well-being if not prosperity. It's safe to say that every member in the tribe of old could effectively participate in the hunter-gatherer life. So could almost everyone be of some use in a farming community. But fitting into the succeeding, print-dependent economies is not for everyone by a long shot. Despite all the hopes for universal literacy, despite the gnashing of teeth while asserting that "it is the birthright of every human being" to be given the opportunity to learn how to read and write, despite pretty well 150 years of compulsory and free education in most countries, the functionally illiterates are

---

[*] "normal" here referring to the norm

with us in the millions, even in the privileged parts of the world. Despite the leveling of most playing fields, far too many players can neither get the sense of a warning notice nor manipulate numbers beyond 4th Grade Math.

Ta da! technology rides to the rescue! Without deep forethought by social scientists or focussed planning by governing bodies, our newest popular inventions have begun to tame the beast of abstractions, that threatening presence that runs along print lines, across life's paths everywhere, even within web-pages. The world will be a much friendlier place—by birthright for real!—for all those who can look.

So, here's looking at **LOOKING**
Looking is the oldest mode of information intake. Before the village encounter, of course, there was the cave encounter. And eons before that, during 14 to 83 million years back, we may have split off the apes. And before that ... The point here is that the eye evolved almost unimaginably long before the organ for listening or the apparatus for talking. That genetic makeup that we share with, say, the reptiles—the eye → brain → action loop—is so old, has survived millions and millions of years of evolutionary adaptation, has become such a marvel of ingenuity that it is the most effortless to use and prompts the most essential reactions. "Aha!", the ever accelerating hi-tech inventions direct themselves toward the business of appealing to the eye; only the occasional bit of print cavorts among the pictures.

Instead of churning out life abstracted in the shape of print, we churn out life represented virtually real in the shape of visuals. As far as we know, our brains began to see three-dimensional, pulsating, colourful life while looking at a two-dimensional likeness of it about 15,000 to 10,000 years—or 750 to 500 generations—ago[*]. We only have to look at the wall-paintings in the caves of Lascaux to marvel at the condensation of a narrative of a hunt onto a flat and limited surface. The eyes take in some lines in two dimensions and the processor, the brain, runs with them and imagines a series of events three-dimensionally. The brain even manages to adjust the colouring! Our central processor has to do considerable work when looking at the hunt painted on the cave wall but not nearly as much as when we ask it to "see", and consequently weep over, Little Nell's death in Dickens' *The Old Curiosity Shop* or the burning of Moscow in Tolstoi's *War and Peace*.

Our fertile, restless brains have, lately, added movement to those two dimensions on the wall. We don't have to imagine the action anymore. We can pay $9.00 in a multi-plex and the screen will do it for us. Soon—can there be any doubt?—the virtual visceral experience of the action will be added. That'll be an alternate mode of looking at and experiencing life. It's a certainty that somebody will "virtualize" the Lascaux cave paintings! Putting on the right head-gear or getting the right implant, manipulating the suitable joy-stick or button will make the consumer of that technology feel the emotions, think the thoughts, and "do" the actions of the Lascaux generations. We generally invent

---

[*] To harp on the glacial pace of evolution: since the time of the Neanderthals, 130,000 years ago in round figures, the human brain has not substantially developed further.

the technology we can imagine. Nevertheless, the imagining and the inventing is done with a brain that is part of a hunter-gatherer body. That body wants to do what it did in the stone age ... but do it technoidally enhanced.

The enhancements tend to get in the way of a steadfast awareness that we operate pretty nearly in the same genetic package as did our stone-age ancestors. We not only prefer but also naturally incline toward their way of life. If our technological brilliance did not blind us, we could see ourselves as creatures of nature, one species in many, no better, no worse. What sets us apart is the capacity of our brain, especially that feature that allows us to think back and to think forward. We are able to regret what we've done now or in the past and resolve to act differently in a future we can imagine—generally the span of one generation, ours! The same brain lets us see ourselves doing something we have not done before.

But, as all animals do, first and foremost we adjust our behaviour in such a way that it maximizes our chances for survival and for putting that 50% of our individual DNA into the next generation. None of this favours the evolution of an inherent need to examine long-term anything. Generally, survival is enhanced when we instinctively bow to the pressure of the environment in which we find ourselves at the moment. To that belongs, of course, the culture of the moment. We want to fit in. We need to fit in. We fit our selves to contemporary cultural unifiers, such as dress, personal hygiene, ways to pass free time.

Print is Toast

To want to fit into the social fabric of the tribe has its roots in survival behaviour from long ago. Because we need to be seen as belonging, we wear and do what the fellow tribe members wear and do. Not homo erectus over their almost four million years, not the Neanderthals in their 200,000, not homo sapiens—at least not until very recently—has been able to survive without others. Cast out from the tribe or lost in uncaring nature, the already short life was doomed to be shorter still. Ergo, it's not been the ornery anti-social type who succeeded in passing on his genetic endowment in large numbers. Figuratively speaking, today we all wear 3rd millennium hi-tech sneakers but we want them to feel as comfortable as going barefoot. As soon as technology allows us to default to the set-points of tribal life, we're off and running in that default mode.

MOST OF THE BIG CULTURAL UNIFIERS TODAY COME IN TRIBAL (CAVE-TIMES) MODE

CLOTHING

Wearing, with minor variations, what others wear at the moment, makes us feel comfortable because we fit in, we belong to the/a group. Because we could not survive alone, we evolved to blend into the crowd. An albino chicken amongst the Rhode Island Reds gets literally picked on to the point of death. A human that really, really fits into none of the "individualized" sub-groups, will live as the eccentric: alone, that is apart from the clump. In dire times, the eccentric is blamed for every mischief that befalls the collective; in good times he/she is uneasily tolerated. We incline quite naturally toward behaving as the group does.

Print is Toast

Our identity is—save for a few harmless "personal" frills—bound up with what the group celebrates, believes, wears.

Once upon a time, a human was clothed in the same casual suit of fur morning, noon, and night. Somewhat later, "casual Friday" was still every day what with leather leggings, woven bark capes, loomed plant fibre or goat hair covering the body. Then agriculture took hold. Women dressed much differently from men; rich folk could be recognized by their finery a mile away. Over time the soldier and the monk, the fishmonger and the servant, even the married and those not yet wedded, could be recognized at a glance. The cachet attached to the distinguishing dress feature—kind of pre-print logo—got so important that recorded history's first wanna-be must have lived in medieval times. So-called sumptuary laws were passed all over Europe. These laws, unenforceable actually, tried to prevent upstarts from using a bow, button, or colour reserved for wearage by the upper classes.

Just before and during the reign of print—which was also the heyday of principalities, states, nations—dress offered geographical information as well. What prevailed is best illustrated by looking at a couple of early 20th century issues of *National Geographic* or a pictorial equivalent. One glance at a photographed person gives enough clues to identify continent, country, state, region, village where she/he lives. As late as in the middle of the 20th century a man or a woman could be pegged to come from within a radius of about 60 kilometres. Their local dress/"costume" advertised that they belonged with the folk in village X.

Print is Toast

Humans are fond of categorizing and sub-categorizing. This ethnic, regional, local finery came variously—though strictly limited—embroidered, buttoned, or sashed to advertise the wearer as unmarried, married, or widowed. Often the material used for a shoe buckle or the colour of a man's scarf broadcast what trade provided him a living.

Wearage got kind of colour- and featureless after that. The industrial revolution's peon and the big organization's man dressed in grey, grey cotton twill and grey wool flannel respectively. During that entire time, if a house door opened, in the frame would stand a woman wearing an apron! Men and women, however, would dress up when they left the house. Men put on a jacket and a hat or cap; women took off that apron and put on coat, hat, gloves. And "Sunday" clothes were for high community or kin occasions: church, assemblies, weddings, funerals. For some reason, the age that prospered because it could, on a large scale, flatten metal and steamroller a lot else was also the age during which womanhood ironed everything in and out of sight. Things were kind of rigid in the dress world. And one was expected to blend in ... rigidly.

Now, with print on the wane and the hi-tech way of earning a living replacing the industrial, clothing becomes more featureless. But also much more comfortable. Much more crinkled. Drip & dry (almost like animal skin). The global tribe pretty well wears the same uniform: some kind of T-shirt, jeans, ball-cap. Our collective foot is shod in pliable running shoes. This get-up is, by the way, much prized by those who have been unable, so far, to go shopping in the (global) village market. We're back where we started: although the Clan of the Cave Bear could be distinguished from the Clan of the Eagle, all clans wore fur. In our time, the clan of the k-locers (k-loc = 1,000 lines of code) at MicroSoft is easily distinguished from the clan of the cubicle-toiler. But all wear casual. And is it wicked to observe that most everyone clued/glued into the Clan of the Globe has pierced and/or tattooed body parts?

COMING OF AGE

Survival of the species, the tribe, the family, the family name, one's DNA becomes possible at the point of physical maturation. Because at this point youths can do the DNA thing and not only herd the goats or shell the peas, specific rituals have throughout time marked the entrance of a young person into adult society. We feel in our gut that some kind of test as well as a celebration should signify the end of childhood. Elders, shamans, lords, the church, even apprentice shops had devised specific ceremonial events to mark this, one of life's milestones. One requirement has held steady over time: that the youth be surrounded by lots of people. The more celebrants are kinfolk, buddies, neighbours, the better. In tribal or early village times, coming of age was serious business. It added a warrior, an artisan, a bearer of children to the community. Earnest and sometimes painful ceremonies were followed by suitable feasting.

By the time print was part of life, coming of age ceremonies atrophied to smaller affairs with family and friends of the immediate family. Confirmation, Bar Mitzvah, Holy

Communion were and are, basically, staid affairs. What was lacking was the bonding thing with and in the midst of many members of one's age-group vis-à-vis the elders. Today, curiously enough, as print loses its grip on the culture, the celebration within the tribe—though this time the peer tribe—again makes its appearance.

At first the great occasion shifted to graduation from high school and to the 21st birthday bash. Although with diminished roles to play, the parent generation was still involved; at the very least they footed the bill. That vast cohort born after 1945 was also the first generation that grew up with mass communication and ever accelerating tech-change. While the young enjoyed the ride, their parents fumbled cruise control.

These teenagers no longer grew into the adult society; instead they grew along with and into their peer-group. They didn't want an established ceremony; they needed a rite of their own. Come the full-blown electronic age, and the defining electronic-digital coming-of-age happening was born. Woodstock is the grand-daddy of them all. It was in that bucolic setting that the urban young established a brand-new ritual for demonstrating that they belonged to the group which would run things in the future. It was the confirmation rite of the Woodstock generation. Ever since, participating in one or more of those huge synergistic events has gotten legions of youths drunk on that ecstatically emotional high of the ultimate "fitting in" experience.

Print is Toast

Today the young who come of age fit in with their peers instead of with the generation of their parents or elder kin. The reason is that the shaping of new tools has speeded up so much that the process has leapt over an entire generation. In the last 25 years, one generation worth of years, it was not the adult generation that invented the defining tool of a new age, the computer; it was those kids in their parents' garages. And the straddling-twentysomethings of the 1970s run the show and the shop.

When they want to talk shop, however, there's no dad or mom to turn to because they're out of the loop. So the signals are taken from the peer group. For the first time ever, the older generation does not teach the young that what defines the adult: job, work, skills to earn a living. Within one generation hierarchies have crumbled, the pieces re-arranging themselves into a network. In a world that's a network—every nodule connected to every other one because the whole thing is a web—the family has permutated as well all over the place. In such a world one comes of age with one's peer group and does not care to measure up to one's elders.

But as initiation rites go, the ritualistic details feel absolutely right. They correspond nicely with those described in studies of primitive tribes which survived into the last century. Here goes: to enjoy a rock concert to the bliss-out stage, one has to suffer (camp out) for the ticket, be jostled to the point of pain by a crushing crowd, have one's senses jumbled by high-decibel amplified tom-tom like rhythmic sounds as well as high-octane yelling by the increasingly ecstatic gathering, light fire (matches) at the same time, consume mind-altering substances, pass some of the faithful in the manner of reliquaries from hand to hand above the heads of one's cohort, feel one with the cosmos, and the next day suffer that sweet afterglow of emotional exhaustion.

CREATURE COMFORT

The stone-age person, incredibly smart but not wise, has pursued ease and plenty from Day One. We, the inheritors and amplifiers of their fancies, live their wildest and most fanciful imaginings because our technology lets us. Here's an example: breakfast. Our really early forebears rolled off their floor mats in the mornings, grabbed some cold leftovers or other edibles and had a drink of water, stored somehow. If nothing had been set by because both hunt and gather had been unsuccessful, they'd have to go forage. In the intervening time between those days and now, that first meal became more varied as well as labour-intensive because agriculture ensured a predictable food supply as well as food storage. Things got a bit out of hand when any one or all of the following started the flow of stomach juices: eggs, bacon, fish, oatmeal, toast & jam, cake, coffee, tea, chocolate. The main point in all this is that even the poorest post-primitive had some stash of vittles, at least the wherewithal to cook porridge, in their dwelling.

However, the higher tech we get, the more we can afford to live like prehistoricals. The first step toward the simple roll out of bed cave routine was the invention of cereal. Doesn't spoil. Doesn't need fire. Needs only one dish.[*] Today hi-tech has combined the one step food-getting with the variety offered on an upper-class sideboard during Queen Victoria's reign. Now that the byte rules, all kinds of forage places and all kinds of feed are close enough to most people's lair. Dedicated coffee brewing locations, 24/7 open convenience stores, gas station coolers, super markets that open at what used to be ungodly times, all serve the rolling out of bed and foraging impulse. The big difference between prehistory and the end of history is, of course, that the modern foraging takes a fraction of the time and that a positive result is assured.

Check it out. Observe what comes to cashiers in the above-mentioned places from about 7:30 to 8:30 early. There's a guy buying nothing but a jar of instant coffee. The mom with two kids goes through with 3 muffins, 2 sandwiches, 2 bananas, 4 juice cartons, 2 cheese & cracker packs, 1 hot coffee. This is breakfast for three, school lunch for two, and mom's wake-up hit. Gender-neutral but first-third-of-life persons tend to put any two of the following on the counter or moving belt: do-nuts, bagels, carton of milk, piece of fruit, M&M bar, yogurt, bag of chips, power bar, container of soy-milk, sandwich from the cooler, box of cookies, a hot coffee. A 40-something male, hair and whiskers as they left the pillow, swipes his card for a loaf of bread, shrink-wrapped ham slices, a litre of freshly squeezed oj, and the coffee he's already drinking. Every cave-person, every nomad, every subsistence farmer should have had it so good!

---

[*] Well, we do brush our teeth. But, honestly, how many of us are tempted to skip that overlay of culture?

EXERCISE

What we now call "exercise" was then what the gatherer, hunter, farmer did all day. No Tiger Balm for them! The concept of exercise did not exist because, whether tribesperson or early villager, one had to "exercise" a lot of body parts to ensure one's continued existence. But an organism that evolved, with exertion being part of the process, needs way more than 500 generations to go by—under essentially the same conditions and in isolation—for any (once upon a time essential) survival behaviour to wither away. So while R&R after exertion was heavenly for those who went before us, we've perfected technology to ensure that heavenly feeling by driving to "work out".

Not enough evolutionary time passed between exercising lots of muscles to procure edibles and our clicking a mouse for a pay-cheque. Any kind of sedentary life is barely 1,500 years old and occupied only a very, very few with copying and illuminating manuscripts, writing histories, philosophies or rhymes, reading, jotting down observations and calculations of a scientific nature, double-entry book-keeping. Despite these novel ways of earning the daily bread, the largest part of any population still sweated the brow. Until well into the 20th century many of those brows were made to sweat by the mechanical machines that set the pace.

Those sweating to put food on the table did not feel the need to jog or rock-climb. It is the ones that invent and use the last few decades' hi-tech, the ones that set the tone of our culture, who return to the "exercises" of veldt, forest, mountain. They feel an overwhelming need to move their bodies in the manner of those who chased the antelope, trimmed sails, carried the wash back from the stream where they had beaten it on the rocks, plowed a field, or worked in the woods. They return to the past so they will feel good in the future. They pay to use cardio-vascular system enhancing machines, they pay to go on Xtreme vacations, they pay to tire their bones digging and planting the perfect garden. They also pay to "gather" bird ID, flower ID, sea shore creature ID. For that they have to roam and hike on their antediluvian two feet. Following your inner Cro-Magnon feels so good!

EDUCATION

Education is a great, if not the greatest unifier. Time was when the older generation shared its knowledge with the next generation. That generation was then bound to the older one by the ribbon of shared information. In tribal times a child was surrounded by a few human beings who knew everything there was to know. All information that existed could be gotten at and fathomed within one's lifetime. The young learned skills via the look-talk-listen route. This was true still in the village in which the cobbler father taught his son to make a decent boot and the champion flax weaver passed on her skill to the daughter. In the country Caleb Miller (though no longer earning his bread by milling flour as, judging by his name, his ancestor did) set an example when he won the plowing contest three years in a row. In the same small community Mary Smith (though her husband took the horse to the smithy, not forged the horseshoe himself) was listened to because she had won the ribbon two country fairs out of five with her intricate embroidery stitched upon her finest, most evenly spun, most flawlessly woven linen.

That was before the rigid lines of writing forced rigidity upon learning and life. At first this new skill was confined to a tiny brotherhood, that of scribes, monks, public clerks. They were the first cerebral workers whose labour tied them to a stool, to a desk, to a piece of parchment. Most in this tiny band of information technicians/processors—the work was either copying or recording of data—had shown a talent for head-work and been taken as small boys away from the parents, tillers of the soil, and the boyhood life of doing adult chores. They were taught by monks within the confines of what was to become the school of today.

Then came the invention of moveable type which allowed owning and studying information in the shape of printed books. From that moment on, the information worker of the future was confined for years to rigid syllabi. The aspiring artisan had to serve long years of indentured apprenticeship which proceeded along pre-scribed stages. Even the unlettered day labourer was tied to someone else's schedule. We're omnivores when it comes to keeping the body alive; we're also omnivores when it comes to keeping our craving for information—new or old—satisfied. Print triumphed over the roving eye because with its 26 letters cast in sufficient blocks to set a folio, information could be caught, tamed, and passed around. Copying speed went up; cost per copy came down.

Print is Toast

Today we catch and tame information into pictures for sharing, and that makes the print lines buckle. Even a modest assembly of books, at most filling a 3 x 2' shelf arrangement, cannot be seen in many living rooms. Yet a radio can be found in almost every room, a TV set in at least two, and a computer in one. Hey! what goes around comes around. It's back to the ancient show, tell, listen mode! The "hows" of manipulating information changes by the half-year. Skills are learned as they are needed. Most teaching is left to the technology of our time: the video, TV, life-style film in school, movies, peer-e-chatting, special interest publications, that which lies behind the portal to the Internet.

The watershed was probably Kenneth Clark's TV series *Civilization* (1969). One man elected himself arbiter of what Civilization was and meant. It was the last hurrah of the printed symbol culture and the first whoop of the electronic mass edutainment experience. Given possession of the same vocabulary, a bright time-traveler from the pre-print past would have been able to get the gist of every televised instalment.

THE WITHERING AWAY OF THE PRINT CULTURE
The day we have to be enticed with a pizza on a checkered table cloth and a glass of wine to buy a cooking pot, that day we know that the food replicator is taking over. On that day cooking, though still practiced, will become a hobby or a status symbol to a relatively few. The food culture as we now know it, will be toast (sorry!). The day the first bookstore greatly enhanced the bottom line because it successfully molly-coddled the stomach and butt of the Cro-

Print is Toast

Magnonite body to entice it to pay for an item that engages solely the brain, that day was the beginning of the end of the print culture. Not the end of the book, but the end of the print culture.

There's nothing ordained or sacrosanct about print. We did without it for many thousands of years. Print will not disappear but already it is no longer the dominant means of communicating anything. Print as a kind of notational input alternative will survive of course. That kind of input-print, however, will not lead to hard copy bound between covers; it will not stir the heart with deep emotion or give one "the shock of recognition". Wisdom, beauty, depth of thought will be experienced visually and aurally.

Wisdom, beauty, complexity is found in the great myths of earth's various cultures. Every one of them came into being and was known by everyone in that particular culture long before moveable type. The New Testament made its points with parables; the Internet, today's "who we are and how to live" bible, offers its revelations through point & click icons. It may sound flippant, but even the greatest story ever told is "only" information. Tech change allows all information that humans possess to pulse through that globe-spanning net while constantly adjusting to our tribal stone-age brains. The Internet did not enter public consciousness until it managed to offer the now ubiquitous graphical interface in place of an array of file names. Besides, once opened, a file would display only text … in Courier typeface yet! Computers did not find a place in our home lives until pointing and clicking replaced the tiresome typing of commands.

Print is Toast

The roaming eye in the service of that Cro-Magnon brain was briefly trained to move in a linear fashion. Wherever print came to be the dominant mode of imparting or getting information, it went straight. Whether from right to left or left to right, top to bottom, no matter: the eye could not roam. Although Gutenberg did his moveable type thing around the middle of the 15th century, print has only been widespread and, therefore, an environment that spawned a culture, for the last 300 years or so. That gives space to about 15 generations, not enough to allow for even a little bit of hard-wired adaptation. On top of asking that one concentrate on the linear, this relatively new way of exchanging information relies on abstract symbols that combine to form words. Although these words are taken in by the eyes, they have to be converted—if that's the right word—to something one can "see" with the mind. Of course this is more labour-intensive, not to say complicated, than just looking, listening, talking.

All messages are a form of narrative. And what matters to our Cro-Magnon brains is the narrative. However, where once the narrative was largely verbal, accompanied by a few gestures (visuals), the narrative now is largely visual, accompanied by a few words. Print presented abstractions, forced the eye to track from left to right successively downward, lacked pictures or sounds, required the learning of skills, and utilized one side of the brain. The narrative on the page, although a glorious and promising achievement, proved merely an interregnum between low-tech and hi-tech **looking** for and at information.

Print is Toast

Information transfer went from show & talk to writing, printing, reading, from that to print with accompanying illustrations. Today the information is on video and other "moving pictures", accompanied by voice-over. Which is the tribal, village mode of information exchange. The improvement is that now what's on tape can be replayed as many times as it takes to "get it". Nobody needs to be embarrassed because they have to ask: "please, show me one more time." The hunter-gatherer in ball-cap and chinos loves to watch some pointers on how to improve his golf swing. And even the HELP advice in computer applications is strewn with little arrow-decorated boxes, a "show me" caption inviting us to click and learn.

The princes of print, for a few centuries the masters of the universe, have been outnumbered and overwhelmed by the commandos of k-loc. It's not so much a defeat as it is a changing of the guard. Already print has been replaced by the icon in daily life: street crossing lights show little walking persons instead of WALK; a hand pops up to indicate STOP (in a print culture four-letter words would not faze anybody!); airports are festooned with long "sign" boards which carry multiple "signs" in the shape of icons. Some of these little pictures—a case of don't fix what ain't broke—are harder to decipher than a six-syllable word with a Latin root.

Other evidence that print no longer rules can be seen when libraries, no longer generously funded, have to *close* for some weeks in order to stay *open* the rest of the year. In one city at least, Vancouver, British Columbia, the replacement technology rode to the rescue. The splendid city library was chosen as a movie location and, thereby, sufficient dollars given over to keep the book stacks open without a break. Print's waning power to rule by appealing to the brain alone can also be seen in the "malling" of the book dispensary. If the vice-president of a bookstore chain praises the growth of audio and video features on his company's web site as "a fantastic way to capitalize on the impulse to buy"[*], then not even offering a licensed bar, pool tables, gourmet coffees and goodies, a garden court yard, and a bistro within the brick and mortar book emporium will re-establish the printed page between covers as something that we are keen to own, use, and cherish.

The *Great Books Video Series* is another tell-tale sign that all is not well with reading. We'd rather spend looking for 126 minutes at *The Age of Innocence* moving by in techni-colour pictures than to follow those black lines in Edith Wharton's slim volume. Every best-seller, every Oprah-recommended novel, many of the so-called Classics are now issued also on audio cassette. And it's a stretch to assert that a book has been read that has been listened to on tape. One cannot make pictures in the head while gardening, watching on-coming traffic, or walking the dog who needs shouting after every twelve seconds. Nor can one concentrate on the finer, what we used to call "philosophical", points another mind is trying to get across to ours.

Print as a commodity is doing well, however. It complements the fare on television and on the Internet. It is

---

[*] National Post, 03.14.2000, p. C 11.

the stuff of and for the tribal life, a life concerned with looking at how other people live or manage their lives. The most consumed print is about concerns of daily life in the village and in the marketplace. TV guides come in print; these schedules are, surely, a consumer item.[*] So is the ever increasing quantity of how-to advice on everything from chucking a bad husband to growing a better tomato, retiring as a wealthy 43 year-old or improving one's memory. Gobs of homilies or 7, 10, 15 steps to self-improvement can be found between covers, fancied up with visuals and set off by overly generous margins. The "distract me please" paperback is doing well and so is the ubiquitous recipe collection.

THE "CULTURE" BOOK WILL SURVIVE

Ideas will still be disseminated through print. And the bookish person will still have a certain authority. Neil Postman[†] will get his wish. He and like-brained persons can enthusiastically, because it comes to them easily, polish off a bit of Voltaire before 12 noon and discuss the philosophical implications of their brainy repast over sour Thai noodle salad at lunch. Postman and his brave band of idea-book readers will still be able to gather "the best that has been known and said"[‡] and try to scatter the human mind's beautiful petals about.

---

[*] " ... TV Guide has 34 million readers [sic] in the US"; Reuters, March 2000

[†] Building a Bridge to the 18th Century : How the Past Can Improve Our Future

[‡] Matthew Arnold; poet, essayist, and school inspector, 1820-88

Print is Toast

The book culture will be, essentially, confined to an elite as it was in the 18th century. That elite—which was a print elite, not necessarily a moneyed elite—met on country estates, in city salons, in coffee houses. In post-print times these book-mates meet in restored 18th century farm houses and are in touch via beautifully phrased, correctly punctuated, abstract thought-heavy e-mail. In those circles Harold Bloom[*] is, indeed, a household word.

But Postman and Bloom cannot persuade, in print, the larger society because that society is not into print; that society is into visuals. The Postmans and the Blooms are not helped by a technology which has set before us more exciting and a greater number of visuals than has any other tool-wielding hitherto. The 5,000 images hitting our eyeballs day after day please and stimulate our made-for-looking neurology. We're pleasure-seeking creatures. And it just so happens that most people get more pleasure from looking at a graphic image than from deciphering an abstract, very spare black image in order to get a handle on an abstract concept. Be it said here that, in the larger scheme of things, the only value attached to either mode of being pleasured is in how far it aids and abets the survival of offsprouts.

With the survival of infants holding steady just a bit below the 100% mark, those inclined toward the book as their information carrier will have their pleasure be someone's profit. Therefore, the "culture" book will survive. However, the book as a number of printed paper sheets bound between covers may well become an antiquarian's staple. But it will

---

[*] whose The Western Canon is much to the point here

have a technological off-spring. Readers will snuggle into their cushioned sofa-corners with their pleasingly textured, comfortably sized, pliable, wirelessly-fed reading tablet. It'll be light as a feather and back-lit for easy deciphering. A light touch on one of the discreetly arranged icons at the bottom will scroll the text down (although, come to think of it, iris-tech is so advanced that the text will probably scroll in sync with one's eye movements). Another icon will book mark, another allow comments to be recorded. Hard on the heels of this "new and improved" version of the book will arise the idea—and the invention follow—that a touch of the VCR icon will play the video of the passage one has just read! This IT embellishment cannot come soon enough. Even the serious 21st century reader is driven to tears of boredom by the sheer quantity of details in Homer's *Iliad* or the narrator's didactic asides in novels of another time. A picture **is** worth 456 words!

The clickable icon has already changed the way we live, work, shop, research, even see reality. This newest tech-tool-toy is no more going to wither away than did the wheel remain a curiosity or the telephone an instrument for distress calls only. That great leveler of the field of opportunities— at least that is how it was seen by many between about 1930 and the late 1970s—the *Encyclopedia Britannica* has put its entire text on the Internet. With falling sales and revisions necessary almost by the month, *The Oxford English Dictionary* has done the same. Besides, running a finger along a printed index or leafing through a fat concordance is no match for the speed with which a search engine produces

a—more often than not even **the**—result. We upright
walkers love speed!

The faster we can sop up information, the faster we can
packrat it into our storehouse. During the evolution of homo
sapiens, over those millions of years, selection was
constantly not only for being open to information but as well
for soaking it up and being able to retain it. Whether a cave-
dweller comes across an "aha!" and makes a mental note of
it, whether a son watches his father use a tool in a unique
way, whether word of mouth or example presents us with
something we haven't come across before, whether a new
experience unfolds before our eyes, or whether we recognize
a new thought in print, whether we bag a factoid with a
mouse-click from the Internet, whether useful or not,
profound or banal, we love to find information. And we love
having that information on tap.

It's a matter of a very foreseeable time when we will carry
the www. universe in our pocket. We'll be able to look at
Internet information by looking at our palm! and the palm-
sized data-enabled wireless cell-phone. That feels so
intuitively right! Get up, step out of the cave, blink at the
light, all information needed to survive is available anytime,
anywhere. What was knowable then was mobile then,
carried in the brain. In our rapid sprint to the global tribal
life the day is not far off when we will hold in the palm of
our hand what is knowable now and then. The cave persons
made voice contact to establish information/news links. We
have the cell-phone. And our palm-pals will recognize our
voices. The scale is wider, bigger, faster though.

Print is Toast

The hunter-gatherer life is not, however, perfection. The hunter runs heedlessly, intoxicated with the chase and the promise of a kill, after the antelope. He gets lost, eventually disoriented, and can not fathom what made him run out of bounds. The gatherer sees yet another bunch of berries on yet another bush yonder. To pack home a praiseworthy haul, she loses direction. In the heat of the pursuit humans tend to lose perspective.

With our short-term vision, cobbled in right at the plant, we are willing to pay serious 21st century money to get our news fix. Yet, we too get lost. Our economy runs on the need for that increased dose to get a high. We pay for information overload. But like the hunter & the gatherer who get disoriented in their quest for what will keep them alive, we don't stop either to consider that

- information does not necessarily communicate
- communication does not necessarily inform
- information, unless relevant to one's endeavour, becomes part of the wallpaper within nano-seconds
- too much information, like too much woolly mammoth meat, will overload the human capacity to digest it
- the information of the day, like the kill of the day, can be stored. However, like the carcass, what's fresh today is starting to look putrid tomorrow.

Humans evolved, prospered, and spread to form a teeming multitude by being news junkies and speed freaks, and by having their brains constantly double-clicking on the "go for it!" button. It's wondrous, though not surprising, to behold how today's technology allows us to make the world once more a fitting place for the hunter and for the gatherer. This most recent, culture-changing, technological invention followed the well-trodden path from down the ages:

- first → putting hard, real material together
- second → using some form of notational instructions
- third → proceeding by looking, doing, talking

So it is that the first computers were metal boxes with manually flickable switches, on-off flashing lights, and just about "hand-wired" circuits. The thing calculated but that was it. Soon came DOS, that cumbersome, hard to learn, print-oriented, letter-input dependent hair-frizzying disk operating system. Considered at the time—less than a generation ago—a big step forward to make the thing user-friendly, the look & grab tool(mouse) produced wysiwyg[*] and the print-based DOS crumpled into dust. Mouse-clicked icons opened sesames on the Apple desktop and, as did the rapidly following Windows3.1 & Windows95, managed to capitalize on that ancient eye → brain → action loop. Steve Jobs, Bill Gates became household names as well as billionaires. Hi-tech refinements clicked into prehistoric behavioural patterns.

We "surf"—that is we roam in the manner of our forebears—for information. We have the same adrenaline dispensers tweaked when we spy our factoid or discover that sprig of useable data. Hi-tech gives both genders equal chances to launch their action from the same pad.

---

[*] "what you see is what you get"

Hunt   hunt the icon, pierce its heart with the arrow cursor; once open, drag the contents home to your very own cave, the c:\ drive stash

Gather   search for the icon, lay it bare with the digging tool, gather (copy) it into your RAM bag, bring (paste) it home

Super-soon we will live a virtual village life. The cord to the generator will atrophy and the line of print fade as we re-enter the wireless world of our millennial past. We'll be able to roam while looking, listening, and talking over vast distances. We'll have more to look at and more to listen to and, definitely, more to talk about.

After that the implant. We will, finally, have succeeded in doing away with that patience-trying fact of evolution taking its own sweet time. As our personal chip encounters changing conditions, our gene structure will adapt. We will be Borg-ified. Humans will live with this *new* technology as they have lived with the *new* tools and toys before the embedded adapter. Fundamentally nothing will have changed because, as the few preceding ruminations may have shown the reader,

RESISTANCE IS FUTILE.

REFLECTIONS

ON THE GLACIAL PACE OF EVOLUTION
AND OUR PLACE WITHIN THAT PROCESS

Rapid tech-change seems the norm to us who live in the 21st century. As these words are being keyboarded and processed by software coded for the task, humans in their 70s and 80s live in our midst who were born into the agricultural way of life, worked for a living in industry, and retired to hike with the aid of a GPS[*], travel around the earth on a metal bird, use a search engine to browse the Internet. Because change is so fast we tend to think that we "evolve" daily. But evolution takes eons. Because it's taken such a long time for us humans even merely to appear on the globe's stage, something needs to be said about big-time T . I . M . E .

We've just celebrated the start of the 21st century. To this event, entirely of our own making, we gave significance by quaffing strong drink and making much noise. Sometime in the recent past it became not only possible but also carried necessity with it to count years. To call a year "Anno 2000" is based on a decision made arbitrarily a few centuries ago and, basically, only means that we've known numbers for a while. To get an inkling of just how short that "while" is, go and look at a banana. Its diameter is roughly the dinosaurs' time; the thickness of its peel is ours. In numbers this means that dinosaurs dominated for more than 140 million years. Upright walkers picked up tool sticks & stones barely 2

---

[*] Global Positioning Satellite

million years ago. Advance to about 36,000 BCE, almost another 2 million years, and homo sapiens sapiens, Cro-Magnon can be seen—still hunting and gathering to survive.

Having read <u>AHA</u>! and taken a look at that most fascinating creature, the information age inhabitant, four particulars regarding our species may be interesting to consider:

1. We are the most adaptable organisms around. We adapt to nearly any environment.
2. During evolutionary times we adapted our behaviour to a certain environment for so long that much of that adaptive behaviour became genetically encoded. That environment has now vanished.
3. We have been around longer than 99.99% of us can really understand (the author included).

Number One
We are the most adaptable organisms around. During our lifetime we adapt to almost any condition, be it slow or rapid in coming. This is the kind of adaptive behaviour that dies with us. In the following example, adaptation existed only as long as the condition prevailed which had caused it. At the turn of the 20th century an Englishman, George Stratton, thought of an experiment[*] which would present the retina with an "upside-down" image of his world. He had himself fitted with a pair of special lenses which made him see everything upside-down by 180° as well as reversed from

---

[*] George M. Stratton, Some preliminary experiments on vision. *Psychological Review*, 1896.

left to right. For the first three days he felt dizzy and bumped into things. After that he could navigate between furniture and even write without pausing. He took his usual evening walk unaided after having worn the spectacles for only one week! What is interesting is that it took the same time to "unadapt" from his downside-up world. In the 1960s a TV camera followed a wearer of such lenses who not only rode a motorbike while seeing the world upside-down but also did some skiing later on while he perceived himself to be hanging by his feet!

As easily and as quickly as Stratton's brain adjusted to the radically altered environment, so have we have adapted to looking through our hi-tech upside-down lenses. We easily live with fast moving steel behemoths, a cacophony of noise, high-speed communication devices, 24 hour shopping opportunities, food on the run. We may grumble but we have adapted to living with polluted air, long life expectancy, making a living by sitting on our butt, being bombarded with 5,000 visual images daily. Equally we take in stride the hundreds of other changes, pleasant or unpleasant, in our living conditions. Presumably we would not have survived as a species if it had not been for this amazing ability to mold our behaviour to whatever nature throws at us or to whatever we choose to invent. I wrote AHA! as a random collection of, as it were, upside-down rides on the bicycle of our invention. Most of the time we don't know that we're riding upside-down; we've adapted ever so well.

Reflections

Number Two
Adaptations can become genetically encoded over many (500 to 1000+) generations. Being adaptable to everyday life and the technology of the day is not the same as gradual, genetic adaptation to environmental conditions over many, many generations. Environment includes human culture as much as it encompasses the desert, the arctic, Mediterranean climes, abundance of wildebeest, 500 generations dwelling close to a fish-bearing river, 750 generations scraping a living from hard-scrabble earth.

The tribal hunter-gatherer "culture" did not change substantially for thousands of generations. Over time and on a non-random basis, those hunters got to be fathers and grandfathers who found their way back to the tribe after chasing the antelope well beyond familiar landmarks. To this day these genetically modified guys are better than women (who didn't hunt and stray off the beaten path) at finding directions.* Today there's a mismatch though. This genetically encoded, magnificent ability is not in sync with the speed and distance a car can put between the erstwhile hunter and his destination. With his make-up selected for being self-reliant as well as stoic when lost, it's against a man's "nature" to ask for directions. For eons there was no one to ask when he had gotten separated from his hunting buddies.

---

* Let's leave my exceptional aunt Betty out of this although it's true that she knew better how to find the shortest way through the woods than any man in the village!

Reflections

It has occurred to quite a few contemporaries that our genetic adaptation to life within a tribe guides, by necessity, our brains' inventions. Hunting, gathering, subsistence farming within an isolated community of 30 to 150 persons sustained us for 99% of our evolutionary past. And it is this thoroughly entrenched survival behaviour fitted for the past which seems to determine what thrives in the arena of popular culture. This wired-in behaviour also explains, for instance, the globe-straddling pursuit of consumer goods. Having pondered a few of our comings, goings, doings I'd go so far as to suggest that for any *thing* or any *pursuit* to be (commercially) successful, it has to tap into feelings, thoughts, actions which are coded into us and have survived from a world which is no more. For instance, we're definitely wired to want to use or own any invention that promises speed. Speed meant survival because it brought success in catching dinner on the hoof, escaping the menacing enemy, or gathering that extra basketful of berries to store for the winter. Today that coding for speed makes us love the hunt and gather on the Internet but also impatient if a download takes longer than 47 seconds.

Number Three
We have been around for longer than we can grasp.
Many, many attempts have been made by brains more excellent than mine to come up with an analogy to illustrate homo sapiens' time-span on ball earth. We've been told to think of an 18" (~ 4,600mm) length of string as representing life on earth. A pitiful 1/10th of an inch (2 mm) of that string is allotted us humans. A bar graph that shows life from the days of the snails leaves humans a sliver so thin that a

magnifying glass is needed to see it. Or we can imagine an enormous bush, drawn in green ink, representing all life on earth from its beginning. Only the tip of one of the leaves could be done in red to represent our kind.

One more time analogy, my favourite one among the many. Spread your arms wide. The tip of your index finger on your right hand is the beginning of life with the first cell divisions. Then look over to the tip of the same finger on your left. That's were we are now. The exact point? The paring of that fingernail! The entire vastness in between shaped us (the evolution of bacteria is the start … the dinosaurs are somewhere in the middle of our right hand). And that immense span of time was devoid of cars, TVs, malls, mechanical noise, clocks, baked bread at the corner store, abstractions, sugar, instant gratification, cows. Even mammals didn't really get going until after the dinosaurs had demised … about 65 million years ago!

Who better to quote before coming to the end of these reflections than the man who started the whole ancestral gene thing, Charles Darwin. Although he kept mostly to turtles, birds, bees, and adaptations of the physical kind in his theory of evolution, he did write this intriguing bit:

> "In the future I see open fields for far more important researches. Psychology will be based on a new foundation, that of the necessary acquirement of each mental power and capacity by gradation." (The Origin of the Species, 1859, p. 449)

Reflections

The key concept "acquirement … by gradation" is not something we short-visioned creatures readily grasp or consider in our daily lives. Whatever took hold genetically to shape our behaviour and mental states did so "by gradation" over the same thousands of generations during which our bodies evolved. Those bodies and minds greeted the third millennium with merry-making and the indispensable gustatory delights. Yet in Year One we did the same. At that time our ancestors greeted the solstice with much yelling, dancing, and drinking of fermented mash. We put the birth of Christ in Year One. That was 100 generations ago.

Only 100 generations. Really!

About the Author

Barbara Parker came to Canada from her native Germany at the age of 23. She learned to speak English while working as a maid; she learned to write her second language by reading a lot and later working in various office jobs. After encountering the usual vagaries of life, she attended Simon Fraser University and earned her MA in English Literature. She taught. More of this and that happened. She returned to office work and retired in the early 1990s.

Other than that, little else can be said about Barbara. She's never published a thing in her life (theses don't count). Going for day-hikes is one of her very favourite activities. Rocks, cedars, arbutus, moss, salal, and views of the ever-changing ocean, integral to the spectacular Westcoast scenery surrounding Victoria, British Columbia, provide peak experiences. In her dwelling Barbara loves to give her electronic "pen" a work-out!

ISBN 155212669-2

9 781552 126691